Longman Handbooks for Language Teachers

Donn Byrne

Teaching Oral English

New Edition

Contents

Preface

Like the first edition of this book, which was published in 1976, this account of techniques and procedures for developing oral skills is intended mainly for teachers and trainee teachers who work in non-privileged classroom situations. Although this book is the product of personal experience and reflection on that experience, it has been the contact that I have had with these teachers, on training courses and in their classrooms, which has largely influenced the content and direction of this book. Through the approach described and illustrated in this book (firmly based on a classroom pedagogy), I have tried to offer teachers both the possibility of comfortably successful language teaching and satisfaction from what they are doing. If they can achieve more, through more daring procedures, so much the better.

In general I have preserved the original structure of the first edition, preferring to modify and expand section and chapter as necessary. Numerous examples of activities have been added throughout, particularly at the production (or free) stage of learning, which has been the most fertile area of development over the last ten years. Some chapters, however, notably the ones on Games, Drama and Integrated Skills, are either completely or mainly new.

Much of the material in this book has appeared in journals in the form of articles. They are: *English Teaching Journal* (Argentina), with which I have enjoyed links for over fifteen years; *Lingua e Nuova Didattica* (Italy); *Modern English Teacher* (UK); *Chalkface* (Japan); *Zielsprache Englisch* (Germany); *Problems and Experiences* (Italy) and *Aula de Ingles* (Spain).

I should also like to preserve in this edition the thanks recorded in the preface to the first edition to Mary Finocchiaro and to Susan Holden and to add my thanks to Jeremy Harmer for scrupulously evaluating the revised edition. My main thanks, however, must go to the many secondary school teachers with whom I have come into contact overseas – whose constant search for self-improvement (often unacknowledged and unrewarded) should provide an example to us all.

1

Language learning in the classroom

1.1
The task of the language teacher

Why is it so difficult to teach a foreign language? To a large extent, it is because we are attempting to *teach in the classroom* what is normally – and perhaps best – *learned outside it*. The classroom is of course a convenient place for imparting information and for developing many educational skills, but our main concern as language teachers is not to *inform* our students *about the language* but to develop their ability to *use the language for a variety of communicative purposes*. In order to develop the skills needed for this, especially the oral ones of understanding and speaking, we have to cope with a number of obstacles, such as:

– the size of the class (often thirty or more learners);
– the arrangement of the classroom (which rarely favours communication);
– the number of hours available for teaching the language (which cannot and should not all be spent on oral work);
– the syllabus itself, and particularly examinations, which may discourage us from giving adequate attention to the spoken language.

Under these conditions it is not easy to provide effective oral practice, especially in large classes. That is why it is important to have a clear understanding and a firm grasp of the wide range of techniques and procedures through which oral ability can be developed. These techniques and procedures are *a way of accommodating language learning to the unfavourable environment of the classroom.*

1.2
The role of the teacher

What, then, is your role as a language teacher in the classroom? In the first place your task, like that of any other teacher, is to *create the best conditions for learning*. In a sense, then, you are a means to an end: an instrument to see that *learning takes place*. But, in addition to this general function (or perhaps we should say in order to implement it), you

1

have specific roles to play at different stages of the learning process. We will look at these stages

– *presentation* (when you introduce something new to be learned)
– *practice* (when you allow the learners to work under your direction)
– *production* (when you give them opportunities to work on their own)

from a conventional standpoint first of all.   .

1.2.1
The presentation stage: the teacher as informant

At the presentation stage, your main task is to serve as a kind of *informant*. You *know* the language; you *select* the new material to be learned (using the textbook normally but supplementing and modifying it as required) and you *present* this in such a way that the meaning of the new language is as clear and memorable as possible (see Chapter 4). The students listen and try to understand. Although they are probably saying very little at this stage, except when invited to join in, they are by no means passive (see 2.1). At this point of the lesson, then, you are at the centre of the stage, as it were! It is a role that many teachers find attractive, and there is a danger of spending too much time presenting (sometimes because you want to make sure that your students have really understood) so that the students do not get enough time to practise the language themselves.

1.2.2
The practice stage: the teacher as conductor and monitor

At the practice stage it is the *students'* turn to do most of the talking, while *your* main task is to *devise and provide the maximum amount of practice*, which must at the same time be both *meaningful and memorable* (see 5.1). Your role, then, is radically different from that at the presentation stage. You do the minimum amount of talking yourself. You are like the skilful conductor of an orchestra, giving each of the performers a chance to participate and monitoring their performance to see that it is satisfactory.

1.2.3
The production stage: the teacher as manager and guide

It is a pity that language learning so often stops short at the practice stage (or at least does not regularly go beyond it). Many teachers feel that they have done their job if they have presented the new material well and have given their students adequate, though usually controlled, practice in it. All the same, no real learning should be assumed to have taken place until the students are able to use the language for themselves, and unless opportunities are available for them to do this *outside* the classroom, provision must be made as part of the lesson. At any level of attainment, from elementary to advanced, the students need to be given regular and frequent opportunities to use language freely, even if they sometimes make mistakes as a result. This is not to say that mistakes are unimportant, but rather that free expression is more important, and it is a great mistake to deprive students of this opportunity. For it is through these opportunities to use language as they wish, to try to express their own ideas, that the students become aware that they have learned something *useful to them personally*, and are encouraged to go on learning – perhaps the most vital factor of all in helping to keep the interest in language learning alive. Thus, in providing the students with activities for free expression and in discreetly watching over them as they carry them out (which is of course one of the best ways of finding out whether the students are really making progress), you take on the role of manager and guide (or if you like, adviser). These are not easy roles either to accept or fulfil, and some of the problems will be examined later (see Chapter 8).

1.2.4
An alternative approach

The sequence described above – presentation → practice → production – is a well-tried approach to language learning which we know to be effective in average (i.e. non-privileged) classroom conditions. It should not of course be interpreted too literally: these stages are not *recipes* for organising all our lessons. In the first place, the actual 'shape' of a lesson will depend on a number of factors e.g. the amount of time needed for each stage. Activities at the production stage in particular can vary a great deal in length. Also, stages tend to overlap and run into one another e.g. some practice may form part of the presentation stage.

However, a more important point is that we need not follow this sequence too rigidly, especially at the post-elementary level, where the students already have a foundation of language. Since our main aim is to get the learners to communicate, we can reverse the sequence outlined above by first setting them tasks which will require them to communicate as best they can with the language at their disposal and then using the outcome as a way of deciding what new language needs to be presented and perhaps further practised. The diagram below shows how we can preserve an essentially three stage view of the language learning process (simply because this is a valuable way of looking at what goes on in the classroom) and yet take a more flexible view.

This model incorporates both the 'traditional' and 'progressive' view of the three stages of learning because we can move either from presentation to practice to production or from production to presentation to practice according to the level of the students, their needs and the type of teaching materials being used.

1.2.5
A key role: the teacher as motivator

So far we have drawn attention to teacher roles that relate closely to the three stages of learning. However, there is one other key role that cuts across these three stages: namely, the teacher as *motivator*. Whatever you are doing in the classroom, your ability to motivate the students, to arouse their interest and involve them in what they are doing, will be crucial. Some key factors here will be your own 'performance' – your mastery of teaching skills, often dependent on careful preparation; your selection and presentation of topics and activities (it may often be necessary to *make* them interesting!) and, of course, your own personality, which in language teaching must be flexible enough to allow you to be both authoritative and friendly at the same time.

1.3
The learners

No class of learners is more than superficially homogeneous, however skilfully it has been formed on the basis of intellectual ability (real or imputed) and language aptitude (or, at the post-elementary level, language attainment). In many classes, especially in state schools, there are considerable differences not only in attainment but also in language skills, aspirations, interests, background and above all, personality. One question is, then: can you afford to ignore these differences? But then we can also ask: why *should* we want to? It is true that we cannot take these differences into account at every moment of the lesson but, unless teaching is viewed as a shaping process from start to finish, these differences need not be either to your disadvantage or to that of the class as a whole. They can in fact be made to *contribute* to language learning in the classroom. Of course we have to make some compromises: this is part of the problem of accommodating language learning to the classroom. Most probably this will be at the presentation stage, where you are selecting and presenting language material for the class as a whole. At the practice stage, too, some things will have to be done with the class as a whole, but here we can begin to take individual differences into account, through pairwork activities, for example. It is at the production stage, however, when the learners will be working for the most part in groups, that individual differences begin to play an important part. The activities at this stage not only *permit* the students to express themselves as individuals; to a large extent, they *depend* on this for their success.

1.4
The needs of the learners

In a few cases, because we know why students are learning a language, we are able to specify more or less exactly what they will need to learn both in terms of language and skills. For most students, however, language learning is a long-term process, with goals that cannot be satisfactorily defined. Often, when they *are* defined, goals are unrealistic, failing to take into account factors such as the amount of time available, classroom conditions (etc.). For many students the only reality is a final public examination with a probable emphasis not on skills that are truly needed but on those that can be measured through a written examination. A poor reward for many years of language learning!

In such circumstances we must try to help the learners in the most realistic way possible. Ultimately, as we have acknowledged, they will need the language for the purpose of communication. How can this best be achieved? First, it is clear that they must master as much of the language system as they reasonably can: that is, its grammar, its vocabulary and its phonology. However, we must at the same time remember:

(a) that learning the language system is not an end in itself; only a means to an end;
(b) that the students do not need to work their way through the 'whole' system (see 1.5). There are many items which they will not need to learn in order to be adequate users of the language;
(c) that learning the language system need not and should not be boring. What we need are ways of giving the learners essential items of language economically and enjoyably.

Secondly, it is equally clear that the learners need opportunities to try out language for themselves: in other words, to experience within the classroom ways of communicating through the language. Here again we must keep certain points in mind:

(a) that communication in the classroom is not quite the same as 'real life' (although the classroom has its own reality). In a sense, everything is contrived or the result of things that have been contrived. This does not mean, of course, that the students will perceive it in this way or that they will benefit less from it.

(b) that communication will often seem a little less than adequate. The students are all the time learning the language as they try it out and, since we cannot postpone these activities which are essential in building up communication skills, we must be satisfied with what they *try* to do and overlook their shortcomings.

These two goals can be summed up by saying that we would like the learners to be able to use the language both with *accuracy* – which depends on mastery of the language system – and with *fluency* – which derives from experience of trying the language out for oneself. Our task, in trying to meet the needs of learners, particularly in non-privileged classroom conditions, is to strike a balance between these two goals so that, in the end, the learners are able to *comunicate adequately*.

In practice, getting this balance is not difficult. There are, on the one hand, activities which clearly contribute to a mastery of the language system and others, on the other hand, which are clearly designed to promote fluency. They belong, respectively, to the practice and production stages of learning, which, from the standpoint of the learners provide the necessary 'ingredients' for communicative adequacy. For we cannot communicate unless we know essential bits of the language system. Equally, these are no use to us if we do not know how to use them appropriately for certain purposes. We can in the classroom, through different types of activities, provide an environment for both these kinds of learning.

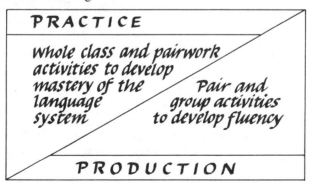

What we cannot know is how different learners will respond individually to these two types of activity and how they will benefit from them. Some, for example, are likely to need more practice in order to master the language system; others may 'pick up' the language system through fluency-type activities. Some, whatever we do, will turn out to be fluent but inaccurate communicators; others will communicate painstakingly and accurately but with modest fluency. Such diversity is typical of an average class of students. By taking a balanced approach we are at least trying to cater for the widest range of needs and, within the constraints of the classroom, giving the learners some opportunities to learn in the way best suited to themselves.

1.5
The nature and role of the syllabus

What kind of syllabus do we want in order to meet the needs of the learners as they were identified in the previous section? There are two main possibilities:

(a) The syllabus may provide us with an inventory of grammatical items (e.g. *in/on/under. What colour ...? can/can't*. Simple Present tense), together with suitable vocabulary, which have been selected and arranged in order according to certain criteria. Great importance is attached to the grading of these items and it is assumed that the learners, following a textbook which embodies the material in the syllabus, will work their way through them in order and that this will be an important factor in helping them to learn the language.

(b) Alternatively, the syllabus may be a list of functions – things that the learners will probably want to do through the language such as advise, persuade, express intentions (etc.) – and notions – the meanings they will probably want to express. These too will be arranged in some sort of order, taking into account both the needs of the learners and the relative simplicity of the language needed to express them (i.e. the exponents).

In addition, the syllabus may contain a list of situations, such as on the telephone, at the station, ordering a meal (etc.), in which the language can be used and a list of activities through which the language can be taught. In practice, both situations and activities are often left to the textbook to provide.

Probably a syllabus which combines these features is best suited to our purpose. It is important to know, especially if we are concerned to develop accuracy, which items of language we have to teach and to have these sequenced for us in an acceptable order. However, one of the faults of traditional structural syllabuses was that they were too detailed and too rigorous, either for the sake of 'completeness' (the syllabus designers were concerned not to leave out any bits of the system) or in order to provide a smooth transition from one item to the next. The result of this was that the learners were not only learning items of language that were of no real use to them but were also discouraged because they felt that they were making little progress. Combining this type of syllabus with functions and notions, on the other hand, can help in the selection of language items because they tell us what use can be made of them.

However, the activities which the learners are asked to perform will probably be the single most crucial factor in determining how well they learn the language. We cannot assume that they will be motivated to learn simply because certain bits of grammar and particular functions and notions are important. They need to *see* this importance and relevance demonstrated. It is through activities of various kinds, both those designed to develop accuracy and those designed to promote fluency that the students are not only able to learn language: they are also able to perceive that they are learning it because they are able to use it.

Discussion

1 Do you agree that your main task as a teacher is to 'create the best conditions for learning'?
2 To what extent do you find the three stages outlined in 1.2 helpful as a way of stating what has to be done in order to meet learners' needs? Would you like to modify them? If so, how?
3 Do you agree that we have to accept that learners will make mistakes at the production stage?
4 Do you agree with the proposal that we should try to get a balance in our classroom practice between accuracy- and fluency-type activities? If you do not agree, what alternatives would you suggest? Would they work in non-privileged classroom situations?
5 What kind of syllabus do you have to follow? Is it satisfactory? If not, how would you like to change it?

Exercises

1 Explain the main differences between the three stages described in 1.2.
2 Make a list of ways in which you try (or would try) to motivate your class.
3 Make a list of a) key structural items b) key functions which you think should be covered in the early stages of a language course.

References[1]

1 On teacher roles, see J Harmer (1983).
2 On language acquisition and language learning, see D Wilkins (1974) Ch 2; L Newmark in C Brumfit and K Johnson (eds.) (1979) and S Krashen and T Terrell (1983).
3 On accuracy and fluency, see C Brumfit (1980) Section 6 and C Brumfit in S Holden (ed.) (1983a).
4 On functional notional syllabuses, see D Wilkins and R O'Neill in S Holden (ed.) (1977). Also K Johnson and K Morrow (eds.) (1984).
5 On syllabus design, see C Brumfit (ed.) (1984).

---

[1]All references are to books listed in the Bibliography on page 138.

2

Oral communication

2.1
The nature
of oral
communication
Oral communication is a two-way process between speaker and listener (or listeners) and involves the *productive* skill of speaking and the *receptive* skill of understanding (or listening with understanding). The diagram below shows how all four skills are related. It is important to remember that receptive does not imply passive: both in listening and reading, language users are actively involved in the process of interpreting and negotiating meanings.

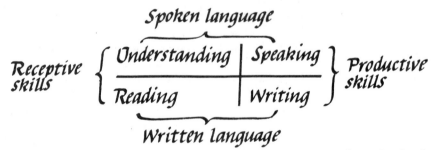

Both speaker and listener have a positive function to perform. In simple terms (because the interaction between speaker and listener is a complex process, see, however, 2.2.3), the speaker has to *encode* the message he wishes to convey in appropriate language, while the listener (no less actively) has to *decode* (or interpret) the message. (It should be kept in mind that the listener's interpretation will not necessarily correspond to the speaker's intended meaning.) The message itself, in normal speech, usually contains a good deal of 'information' that is redundant (i.e. it contains more information than the listener actually needs in order to understand, so that he is not obliged to follow with the maximum attention. See 3.1). At the same time the listener is helped by prosodic features, such as stress and intonation, which are part of the meaning of the spoken utterance, as well as by facial and bodily movements such as gestures. We should also note that, in contrast to the written language, where sentences are usually carefully structured and linked together, speech is often characterised by incomplete and sometimes ungrammatical utterances, and by frequent false starts and repetitions.

**2.2
Pedagogical
implications**

Clearly we have to devote a high proportion of class time to developing oral productive skills. However, understanding, or listening, simply cannot be left to take care of itself. Consider what will happen when the learners try to use the language for themselves outside the classroom, where they no longer have any control over what is said to them. Understanding breaks down almost immediately. Furthermore, poor understanding often results in nervousness, which will probably in turn further inhibit the ability to speak.

2.2.1
Listening
comprehension

The first point to be appreciated is that it is simply not sufficient to expose the learners to those samples of spoken language (dialogues or teacher talk) which have been simplified to provide the students with models for oral production. There are two main reasons why these are inadequate:

(a) the learners' ability to understand needs to be considerably more extensive than their ability to speak (as in the mother tongue). While it is clearly impossible to specify how much greater our receptive knowledge needs to be, the diagram below should help to remind us that, in order to be 'comfortable' in a foreign language – and therefore to be able to communicate effectively – the learners will need a broad receptive 'base'.

(b) the samples of spoken language in the coursebook, which have been skilfully contrived as models for oral production, do not usually contain a sufficiently high proportion of the features of natural speech which we noted in 2.1 (e.g. hesitations, false starts etc.). Utterances tend to be carefully structured and complete (because they are, on one level, written texts), and the level of redundancy is generally low. Therefore, although it is generally agreed that models of this kind are effective for developing productive skills, especially at the beginning level, the learners will need much more than this if they are going to be able to cope with real-life language situations. They will need, in short, a listening comprehension programme which will expose them to suitably varied models of natural speech – and this programme should start as early as possible in the language course. To sum up, the learners have to be *taught* to listen as well as to speak.

2.2.2
Oral production

The main goal in teaching the productive skill of speaking will be *oral fluency*. This can be defined as the ability to express oneself intelligibly (see 2.3), reasonably accurately and without too much hesitation (otherwise communication may break down because the listener loses interest or gets impatient). To attain this goal, you will have to bring the students from the stage where they are mainly imitating a model of some kind, or responding to cues, to the point where they can use the language freely to express their own ideas. (Note, however, that these two processes should be going on all the time, side by side, although the proportion of controlled speech to free speech will change as the course progresses. See the diagram below.)

You will therefore need to give the students two complementary levels of training:

(a) practice in the manipulation of the fixed elements of the language (phonological and grammatical patterns, together with vocabulary);
(b) opportunities for the expression of personal meaning.

In effect, we come back to the two notions of accuracy and fluency, which were mentioned in 1.4. Their relative importance, in terms of the amount of attention we need to pay to them at different stages of the language programme, may be represented diagrammatically as follows:

E L E M E N T A R Y

Focus on accuracy	*fluency*

A D V A N C E D

accuracy	*Focus on fluency*

2.2.3
Interdependence of oral skills in communication

Although in the classroom situation it is often necessary to concentrate at certain times on developing one of the oral skills rather than the other (e.g. part of the lesson may be given over either to speaking or to listening), we must not lose sight of the fact that oral communication is a two-way process between speaker and listener. The diagram below shows what happens in a speech situation and incidentally, therefore, what is involved in oral ability.

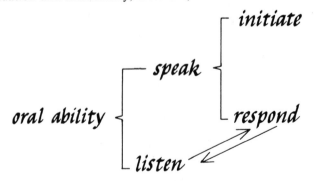

Thus, in some situations one person may do all the speaking, as for example in a lecture. Here, typically, the speaker initiates and simply keeps up the flow of speech. This also happens sometimes when a person is giving instructions or directions. Normally, however, as in a conversation, although one person *initiates*, speaker and listener are constantly changing roles (see 3.1.1) and consequently speaking involves responding to what has been heard. In this case, *speaking is an integral part of listening*. It is this particular kind of interaction (listen-respond-listen etc.) which is difficult for the learners.

In the classroom, therefore, you will need to ensure that the two skills are integrated through situations that permit and encourage authentic communication (e.g. especially through talk and discussion in small groups) and also that the learners are taught how to keep the channel of communication open in such situations (e.g. by asking for repetition and clarification; by interrupting; by signalling agreement or disagreement etc.).

2.3
Intelligibility

Intelligibility is conventionally defined in phonological terms (e.g. being able to make the difference between key sounds such as /iː/ and /ɪ/. At the level of basic understanding, this aspect of intelligibility is unquestionably important but, for the purpose of oral fluency, the term needs to be extended to include mastery of other areas of language. For clearly, in order to be able to communicate effectively, the learners also need an adequate mastery of grammar and vocabulary. Thus, in most language programmes, the amount of time available for systematic speech training is bound to be limited: it will be necessary to concentrate on essential features such as the differences between key sounds, weak forms, basic stress and intonation patterns, and even here more attention will need to be paid to reception than to production. On the other hand, students probably need to be given more vocabulary than their textbooks provide, partly because they feel the need for this themselves and partly because inadequacy in this area often causes communication to break down.

2.4
Oral ability and motivation

The development of oral ability is a good source of motivation for most learners. Here are some points to pay attention to:

(a) *Try to find ways of demonstrating to the learners that they are making progress in the language all the time.* You can do this, for example, by repeating an activity from time to time (such as a game or a discussion), so that they can see for themselves how much more language they can use.

(b) *Ensure that controlled practice, when you will monitor and want to correct the learners' performance, is matched by opportunities for free expression,* when the learners should not be discouraged by correction. Learners are always motivated when they find they can actually do something with the language. (Equally, of course, they can be discouraged when they fail, so activities may have to be selected, especially in the early stages.)

(c) *Show the learners how to make the best use of the little they know.* Sometimes they cannot express an idea because they do not have the precise language they have in mind. They need to be shown how to get round these difficulties through paraphrase and alternative expressions.

Finally, we should accept that some learners will never achieve a high level of oral proficiency. We all know this, as teachers – and yet we still expect all our students to excel in the same way. Overall, we should be satisfied if the students reach *a high level of comprehension* (since this is essential for oral communication) and *an adequate level of production*. By placing more emphasis on comprehension we are also identifying a goal which is attainable with large classes (especially if you expose your students to a good deal of language e.g. by talking to them yourself, using recorded material etc.) and will therefore motivate the majority of the students.

2.5 Oral ability through integrated skills

So far we have talked about oral ability as if it were something that we developed in isolation in the classroom. Normally, however, this will not be the case. If we are looking for sources of talk, whether guided or free, it is apparent that many of these will come from reading and writing activities. Students will, of course, need dialogues as conversational models but these are not necessarily the best stimulus for talk. A reading text on an interesting or relevant topic may be much more productive, often because the ideas are presented more directly. Through reading the learners can also greatly expand their receptive knowledge of the language (see 2.2.1), especially in the often neglected area of vocabulary. Similarly, a writing activity, done collaboratively in pairs or small groups, will be accompanied by a good deal of talk – talk that is needed to *get something done*. Other examples of integrated skills activities are given in Chapter 11.

Discussion

1 Do you agree that the learners need to be *taught* to listen?
2 Do most syllabuses (and textbooks) pay enough attention, in your opinion, to receptive skills?
3 What steps would you take to see that the learners develop a 'broad receptive base'?
4 Suggest some reasons why you think oral proficiency would be important for the average learner? Which would have immediate motivational value?

Exercises

1 Examine any textbook to see what steps are taken to develop oral fluency.
2 Examine some examples of written language and make a list of the ways in which sentences are linked together.
3 Suggest at least two different ways in which a change of stress and intonation pattern would affect the meaning of each of the following:
   (a) I don't find it very interesting.
   (b) Of course, not everyone is as rich as she is.
   (c) Do you really think so?
4 Examine some textbook dialogues to see what attempt has been made to incorporate some features of natural speech.

References

1 On the four skills, see H G Widdowson (1978) Ch 3 and J Harmer (1983) Chs 5 and 9.
2 On oral ability, see D Byrne in S Holden (ed.) (1983a).
3 On speech and writing, see D Byrne (1979) Ch 1.

3

Listening comprehension

3.1
**Listening in the
mother tongue**

We have noted (2.1) that listening is essentially an active process. Yet if we are listening to something in our mother tongue, understanding normally seems effortless! There are a number of reasons for this. First, our experience of the spoken language is enormous, going back to the time we were born. We have been exposed not only to vast quantities of language, but also to a wide range of speakers, varieties, topics (etc.). Because of this experience of language we are immediately able to identify and select those elements in the message – phonological and grammatical patterns as well as lexical items – which are, or seem to us to be, the most important and we are able to retain these in our short-term memory while we continue to listen. Secondly, again because of our experience of language, and also because of our awareness of other factors too (see below) we are normally able to predict what is likely to come next, so that listening is often a confirmation of what we have already anticipated. Thirdly, we normally have a number of contextual clues to help us: we know (either because we can see for ourselves or because we have been told or because we can guess) something about the *participants* (sex, age, status, relationship to one another etc.); the *setting* (where language is being used); the *topic* (what the speaker or speakers are talking about) and the *purpose* (why language is being used). On the basis of all this we are able to make further predictions and respond appropriately.

Of course not all listening situations are easy, even for native speakers. We sometimes experience difficulties when we cannot see the špeaker(s) – particularly facial expressions – as on the telephone, for example. Certain varieties of the language and certain topics make understanding more difficult and require us to concentrate harder. And sometimes the length of time we are required to listen for, without participating, may cause memory problems or even fatigue, so that in the end we simply no longer listen with understanding.

**3.1.1
Listening and
responding**

It will be helpful at this stage to take account of the two main ways of responding to something we have heard:

(a) *interacting*: that is, the listener also participates as a speaker in, for example, a conversation or discussion. This happens in even the simplest conversations: e.g.

A: What shall we do tonight?
B: Don't know. Why don't we just stay at home?
A: All right. I thought you might like to go out, though.
B: Not really. Unless you do.
A: No, I'd quite like to stay in for once.
B: Let's do that, then.

A and B are thus continually changing roles and the interaction cannot be sustained unless they *listen to each another*. Interacting is probably the commonest form of listening, at least in everyday behaviour.

(b) *reacting*: that is, the listener does or says something *as a result of* what he has heard but is not involved (at any rate immediately) in an interaction with the speaker. This situation is similar to reading, because the listener is 'distanced' from the speaker. Here are some examples:

(i)   You are at the airport. You hear an announcement that your flight has been delayed. Reaction: you . . . go and have a coffee/ask for more information . . .

(ii) You are intending to go for a walk. The weather forecast on the radio says that it is going to rain. Reaction: you . . . change your plans/put on a raincoat/ . . .

(iii) You are on a bus. You overhear two people talking about something they have read in the paper. You . . . tell a friend what you heard/buy the newspaper and read the article yourself/ . . .

Reactions, by their nature, are typically open-ended and non-predictable. They may of course lead on to interactions (for example, at the airport, you may grumble with a friend or go and complain. Asking for more information will also be an interaction).

**3.2
The situation of
the learners**

In contrast to the situation described in 3.1, the learners have considerable difficulties to face. In the first place, their experience of the language is very limited. In the early stages, they may still be mastering basic phonological and grammatical patterns as well as vocabulary, all of which the native speaker understands so effortlessly. Inevitably, therefore, they are obliged to concentrate much more and will probably have difficulty in selecting and retaining key items. Secondly, unless they are engaged in talk either with you or with fellow students, they cannot interact: they must listen, often for longer than is natural, and they must react, usually in response to a task which someone else has determined for them. Finally, in most typical listening situations in the classroom, the learners are deprived of a whole range of contextual clues while they listen: they cannot see the speakers (their faces and their gestures) and they have to remember who is speaking, or the setting – unless of course video is being used. Most of the time they are like people listening outside a window to a conversation going on in a room between people they cannot see!

**3.2.1
The needs of the learners**

From what has been said in 3.1 and 3.2 it may be felt that we can best meet the needs of the learners by replicating the mother tongue situation as closely as possible in the early stages of the language programme: that is, by exposing the learners to as much language as possible without requiring them to speak. There are, however, two main objections to such an approach. In the first place, this only superficially reproduces the mother tongue situation, where we know that children learn through interacting with their parents and other speakers. We cannot determine the value of the preceding period, when at a younger age children are simply listening. Secondly, the classroom, with a large number of students brought together for a short time, is a totally different language learning environment: we cannot expect the learners to sit and listen for long periods on the grounds that this will be good for them in the long term. (In any case, children learning their mother tongue do not *sit and listen!*)

However, we can learn from the mother tongue experience. Apart from extending the scope of the listening comprehension programme (along the lines indicated in 3.3) and treating it firmly as an integral part of the oral skills programme at all times, we should be cautious about forcing learners to speak before they are ready (especially when new language is being presented) and we should not demand, when they do speak, that they are accurate from the start. Accuracy is something that most learners attain only with time.

**3.3
The purpose and nature of the listening comprehension programme**

The following main goals are suggested for the listening comprehension programme:

(a) *to give the learners experience of listening to a wide variety of samples of spoken language.* The purpose here, then, is *exposure* (as in the mother tongue) to:
   - different varieties of language (standard/regional, formal/informal etc.);
   - different text types (conversational, narrative, informative etc.).

   The motivation for the learner should be pleasure, interest, and a growing confidence at being able to understand the spoken language without reference to the written form.

(b) *to train the learners to listen flexibly* e.g. for specific information, for the main idea or ideas, or to react to instructions (i.e. by doing something). The motivation for this type of listening will come from tasks, which are interesting in their own right, and which will focus the learners' attention on the material in an appropriate way.

(c) *to provide, through listening, a stimulus for other activities* e.g. discussion, reading and writing.

(d) *to give the learners opportunities to interact while listening.* In the classroom this must be done largely through discussion-type activities and games, where listening forms a natural part of the activity. This type of activity will be done mostly in small groups, but there are occasions when the teacher can profitably interact with the whole class.

3.4
Activities and procedures

The list below gives examples of some of the activities which can be used to implement the guidelines suggested in 3.3.

3.4.1
'Exposure' listening

The material for this will consist mainly of:

(a) *Stories, anecdotes, jokes, talks, commentaries* (i.e. with one speaker only)

Most learners need practice in listening to material with a single speaker only, so that they do not have the added difficulty of trying to identify the speakers when they cannot see them). The material may be recorded or improvised by the teacher. If you are telling a story or giving a talk to the class, try to be as spontaneous as possible (i.e. use outline notes rather than read a script).

(b) *Conversations, discussions, plays* (i.e. with more than one speaker)

The students will need to be given some background e.g. about the speakers. For plays they may actually need to follow the written text.

(c) *Songs (both traditional and pop)*

These provide a good form of listening because the students are generally very much concerned to make out the words. It can of course be combined with some form of task (see d) in 3.4.2 below: the students can be asked to fill in missing words, phrases or sentences or could be asked to relate what they hear to a script that is unclear in some way (e.g. because it is faded).

(d) *Videos and films*

Clearly there is great advantage in using wherever possible recorded material where the students can *see* what is happening (even if it is only two people talking) as well as listen.

Note that by listing these items in this section it is not implied that there cannot or should not be any related tasks or follow-up work. Students may well like to try to write down the words of a song (see 3.4.2 d), which could begin as an individual task and then lead on to a collaborative group activity. In fact, any of the activities listed above may lead on to class or group discussion or to writing. However, the main aim is to provide pleasurable listening as an end in itself.

3.4.2
Task listening

The number of possible activities here is virtually limitless, although it is intended that the list below covers key areas.

(a) *Ear-training*

In distinguishing between key sounds, stress and intonation patterns. Most learners need, enjoy and will benefit from activities which will help to improve their receptive ability in these areas, especially if they are presented in a game-like way (e.g. through team competition).

(b) *Game-like activities*

'Simon says' and variations on the game of 'Bingo' are effective ways of getting learners to respond to instructions, listen out for specific items and so on. Many language games depend for their success on students listening carefully to one another.

(c) *Instructions*

Activities such as picture dictation, where the students have to draw a picture which the teacher (or another student) talks about without showing them; completing a map or picture; following a route on a map in order to arrive at a particular place; arranging objects (e.g. pictures on an outline scene), involve careful listening without requiring a verbal response (unless the listeners ask for clarification).

(d) *Completion-type activities*

For these the students have an incomplete version of a story, a description or a song (words, phrases or sentences omitted) which they have to complete either while they listen or afterwards.

(e) *Identifying mistakes or contradictions*

For example an object (thing, person or place – either real or in pictorial form) is described and the students have to listen and note down any mistakes. Similarly a text (a story or description) containing internal contradictions can be used for the same purpose.

(f) *Finding differences*

The students hear, for example, two versions of a story or two accounts of an event (e.g. an accident) and have to identify the points of difference.

(g) *Problem-solving*

For example, the students are shown pictures of 3–4 people, places, events (etc.) and listen to one of these being described. Their task is to decide which item is being talked about. Students may also be asked to categorise on a worksheet items mentioned in a conversation or discussion. For example, in a conversation about school:

SUBJECTS	SPORTS	CLUBS
history maths physics	football	drama

(h) *Extracting information*

This is probably one of the commonest types of listening tasks. For this the students will probably need a chart of some kind (similar to the one above) which they have to fill in according to specific instructions. For example, if they are listening to a broadcast they may be asked to note down the main topics or, on an easier level, decide in what order they occur in the talk. For example, in a talk about a town, the students may be given the following instructions:

facilities		The speaker deals with the following features of the town. As you listen, put a number against each item to show the order in which he does this.
industries		
location		
other features		
population		

This activity is an effective way of getting the students to impose order on a text which they have heard before they are asked to carry out other tasks which also involve extraction of information, such as answering questions.

For tasks which involve extracting information it is often desirable to define the role of the listener so that he has a clear purpose for carrying out the task. For example, if the listening text consists of a conversation between two speakers discussing a shopping expedition, ask the students to identify with one of the speakers and make notes in the form of a shopping list.

**3.4.3
Listening as a stimulus to other activities**

Note Many of the activities mentioned in the previous section could lead on to pair- or groupwork if for example, the students are asked to compare and discuss their answers. The activities in this section differ in that they are specifically designed to lead on to activities involving other skills.

(a) *Jigsaw listening*

As its name implies, the basic mechanism underlying this activity is that the information needed to complete a task (such as attending a meeting) has been shared out between 3–4 groups in the class. Each group listens to its own piece of recorded material and notes down on a worksheet the information available. The groups then combine to pool their information.

(b) *Ambiguous conversations*

The students hear a short conversation (or an extract from a long conversation), which provides very few clues as to what the speakers are talking about. The students themselves have to decide who the speakers are, where they are, what they are talking about and, possibly, what will happen next. This type of listening then, leads on naturally to discussion (and, if desired, writing).

(c) *Decision-making*

The students are given some information e.g. about a town (places of interest, facilities etc.) in the form of a talk or conversation, on the basis of which they have to plan a visit. The planning involves discussion and note-making. Decision-making activities can also involve, for example, making choices between places, events, activities, for which the background information is made available in recorded form.

(d) *Pre-reading activity*

The students hear, for example, a conversation about the Loch Ness Monster, as a stimulus to reading an article or book on the subject. Similarly they can be asked to listen to short reports on books (e.g. graded readers from the class library) before deciding which one they want to read.

(e) *Pre-writing activity*

This can be in the form of a communication game, similar to *Describe and draw* (see 9.3.1). One student describes a picture which the others in the group are not allowed to see. The students who are listening make notes (and can also ask questions if they want more information). They then use these notes to write a description of the picture.

3.4.4
Interactive
listening

Most interactive listening situations will be in the form of discussions and games, as indicated in (a) and (c) below. Two important points need to be kept in mind.

First, these activities form the basis of oral work at the production stage (see Chapters 7 and 8), where the emphasis is on getting the learners to use language for self-expression. It should not be forgotten, however, that listening is an important aspect of these activities. The learners *have* to listen in order to participate.

Secondly, although these activities will normally be done in groups, in order to give the students themselves as many opportunities as possible to use language, you should also look for suitable opportunities to interact with the class as a whole, through conversation, discussion, and games. While it is true that you cannot have a 'normal' conversation with a class of twenty to thirty students, your interaction with only a limited number of them may be their only opportunity to experience language used by a proficient speaker which has been adjusted to suit their needs and interests. This must be regarded as a significant component of the listening comprehension programme.

(a) *Discussion-type activities*

These provide good listening practice because they get the students to listen to one another, especially if the discussion is geared towards making a decision of some kind. For example, the students may be asked to plan a park, improve the facilities in their home town, solve traffic problems (etc.). For such activities the students have to listen to one another in order to participate. See Chapter 8 for other examples.

(b) *Predictive listening*

For this activity a text (e.g. in the form of a short dialogue) is read aloud sentence by sentence. The students are asked to interpret the sentence and to predict what they think will follow. As the text builds up, they can revise their interpretations. Although this is a contrived activity, it encourages very careful listening both to the text itself and to the various interpretations suggested.

(c) *Communication games*

Many communication games (see 9.3.1) provide excellent listening practice. See, for example, *Describe and draw* where the listeners, whose task is to draw the picture being described, interact with the speaker in order to elicit more information. *Complete it* is based on the jigsaw principle. In this case, however, the information is divided up *visually* among the participants (e.g. each one has part of a story sequence), who have to talk and ask questions in order to build up the complete story. Games which involve the evaluation of a player's performance, such as *Use it*, also provide purposeful listening practice.

(d) *Interviews*

The students can be asked to design questionnaires or surveys, which they then use to interview one another or people outside the classroom. Interviewing of this kind involves careful listening and recording of answers.

3.5 Authentic or non-authentic material?

There is no short satisfactory answer to this question. The important point, as always, is to meet the needs of the learners. On a short-term basis the learners need to listen to material which allows them to feel comfortable, perhaps because it is mainly recycling known language. In addition to this, particularly taking their long-term needs into account, the learners have to be exposed to listening material which is beyond their productive level. Whether this is 'authentic' in the early stages is not entirely relevant provided the material gets them used to *not understanding* every word (and *not expecting* to understand it); encourages them to *guess* – and, over and above this, stimulates them to talk (or read or write, if these are follow-up activities). But, of course, whenever possible, some authentic material should be used, and on an increasing scale as the course progresses. However, it must be kept in mind that the use of authentic material for listening is very different from reading, where, because the learners can work individually and at their own pace, authentic material carries fewer risks. In the typical listening situation, care has to be taken to see that learners are not discouraged by excessive difficulties. In general, *authentic materials are best used where the learners themselves are likely to appreciate them and accept them in spite of difficulties.* One such area is that of pop songs, where the learners are rarely put off by difficulties – and hardly ever taken in by the pseudo-product.

3.6 Dictation

Listening comprehension need not involve any overt responses on the part of the students (in fact it has been suggested that often you need only check *informally* to see whether the students have understood). Dictation, on the other hand, does: it involves the ability not only to understand a sequence of sentences read aloud but also to reproduce it in writing. It is a more difficult exercise than is generally appreciated, even when the text is made up (as it normally should be) of patterns and vocabulary which the students are familiar with both in their spoken and written forms. Admittedly, in order to allow the students time to write, the text is divided up into smaller units (i.e. sense groups based on sentence, clause and phrase boundaries), although this only adds to the artificiality of the exercise. The problem is, then, how can we make it more purposeful?

In the first place, we might use dictation to focus attention on specific problems of pronunciation. For this purpose you may dictate not a passage but a number of sentences that contain, for example, minimal pair distinctions (e.g. *Will you buy me some pepper when you go to the shop?/Go to the shop and buy me some paper*). In this way the students are required to listen carefully to *complete* utterances and to write them down, taking the differences (e.g. *pepper/paper*) into account. Similarly, sentences for dictation may provide practice in distinguishing between homophones (*bored/board, see/sea* etc.) which the students listen to in context: for example, *He got bored in the end* and *He got on board in the end*. This is basically a test of understanding rather than spelling, although of course the students must also know the correct orthographic form for each word.

Secondly, if passages are used for dictation, they should in general not only be short but also to a large extent contain sentences that do not have to be broken up into units that are meaningless when heard separately. A sentence such as the following, for example, cannot be satisfactorily divided up into sense groups: *The inspector sat in his office, studying the reports on the three people who might have stolen the colonel's collection of rare coins.* It is better therefore to present it to the students in the form of much shorter sentences, each of which will be meaningful to them when they hear it. For example: *The inspector sat in his office. He was studying the reports on three people. Any one of these might have stolen the colonel's collection of rare coins.* Although the last sentence is perhaps still too long, it would be better to repeat it two or three times rather than divide it up.

An *authentic setting* may be provided by presenting the dictation in the form of a letter (including the address, since this is an item which we are often required to write down in real life). In this form the exercise becomes less impersonal and the texts used for this purpose may include sentence types (questions, commands) which are less commonly found in other types of passage. To add another purpose to the activity, the students may be asked to supply the punctuation themselves (which is normally dictated when the exercise is used as a test). The discussion of this afterwards must, of course, be conducted on a common-sense basis.

Discussion

1 Do you agree with the importance attached to developing listening skills?
2 Do you think it is important to use authentic materials for listening as early as possible in the language programme?
3 What is your view of the value of dictation?

Exercises

1 Suggest some types of listening comprehension material which would be suitable for: (a) children (b) adolescents (c) adults.
2 Examine any textbook to see what provision for teaching listening comprehension skills has been made. In your opinion, is it adequate?
3 Suggest other activities for each of the four sections in 3.4.
4 Choose some songs ('pop', folk, traditional) which you think would be suitable for inclusion in a listening comprehension programme. Give your reasons for choosing them.

References

1 On listening comprehension in general, see P Ur (1984) Chs 1 and 2. Numerous examples of activities are given in the following chapters.
2 On the spoken language, see G Brown (1977). Also G Brown and G Yule (1983).
3 On interaction, see R Ellis (1984) Ch 5.
4 For examples of listening comprehension activities, see:
   – H Moorwood (ed.) (1978) Section 4;
   – J Willis (1981) Ch 18;
   – G Abbott and P Wingard (1981) Ch 3;
   – M Geddes in K Johnson and K Morrow (eds.) (1981);
   – P Hubbard et al (1983) pp 79–91;
   – S Holden (ed.) (1983b) Section 2;
   – A Matthews et al (eds.) (1985) Ch 5.

4

The Presentation stage

4.1
The presentation of new material

It was pointed out in 1.2.1 that one of your roles as a language teacher is to present new material: that is, to teach the meaning of new items which the learners will need in order to extend their mastery of the language. There are different ways of doing this – through texts, activities or situations – but, whatever approach you use, the procedures must be:

(a) *economical*: because understanding is only part of the learning process and you must not spend too much time on this stage;

(b) *effective*: otherwise the students will not understand what they are subsequently required to practise.

Since many coursebooks rely heavily on texts (dialogues or passages) as the framework for presenting new items in combination with previously learned material, we will look at this approach first. Alternative ways of presenting new language are considered in 4.5.

4.1.1
The function of the text

If the new items are being presented within the framework of a text (a dialogue or prose passage. See 4.2), in combination with previously learned material, your main concern will be to exploit the linguistic context presented in this way to the best advantage. The text, therefore, is a means to an end – getting the learners to communicate by *mastering the rules which are embodied in it* – not an end in itself. For this reason there is little point in getting the learners to learn it by heart, either as a whole or in part. No amount of sentences learned in this way will lead to mastery of the language. Once they have 'extracted' the rules and learned to use them for themselves, the text is of no further importance. Your main task, therefore, will be to focus attention on relevant items of language so that the rules are learned.

4.2
What type of text: dialogue or passage?

Our main concern in the early stages of the language programme will almost certainly be the teaching of the spoken language, and for a number of reasons dialogues would seem to be best suited to this purpose:

(a) they present the spoken language directly in situations in which it is most commonly used;

(b) they permit and encourage the learners to practise the language in the same way;

(c) they encourage active participation in the lesson.

In contrast, prose passages (narrative, descriptive, informative) appear to have none of these obvious advantages. By way of compensation, however:

(a) they can be used to introduce language items which do not fit naturally into conversational-type texts;

(b) they can provide material for learners to talk about: e.g. informative texts can be used to present interesting and educationally valuable topics;

(c) they offer variety.

They also provide incidental reading practice, which is now accepted as an important goal, even in the early stages of a language course.

For these reasons, therefore, we can expect most coursebooks to offer a judicious combination of both types of text. Our task is to make the best use of them according to the needs of the learners.

4.3 Presenting dialogues

These criteria are intended to help you evaluate the dialogues in your coursebook. They may also serve as guidelines if you want to write supplementary material of your own.

4.3.1 Some criteria for evaluating dialogues

(a) *The language should be relevant.* That is, the main items (grammatical or functional) should be ones that will really help to build up the learners' ability to communicate.

(b) *The language should be appropriate.* That is, the language should use forms which are typical of the spoken language (e.g. contracted forms, short form answers, hesitation markers etc.).

(c) *The situations should be realistic and relevant.* That is, the dialogue should create the impression that the speakers are *real people in a real world, using language for a purpose*, not simply exemplifying bits of language. The situations and characters must of course relate to the needs and age of the learners. Children and adolescents are more likely to be motivated by an 'adventure' – type situation, while adult learners are more likely to value 'survival' – type situations such as travel, shopping, looking for accommodation etc.).

(d) *The structural or functional items should be limited.* That is, the dialogue should concentrate on presenting one or at the most two main items. (Other related items, particularly other exponents of a function, can be added at the practice stage.) You should expect the item(s) to be adequately exemplified in the dialogue, but not repeated so often that the language sounds unnatural.

(e) *The lexical items should be limited.* The dialogue is not a suitable vehicle for teaching a lot of vocabulary. Additional items can be worked in at the practice stage. (Note, too, that prose texts will often accommodate a good deal of vocabulary quite naturally.)

(f) *The dialogue should not be too long*. A convenient length (taking into account the way it will be presented and practised in class) is about 8–10 exchanges (though obviously much will depend on the situation).

(g) *The dialogue should be interesting*. The students are more likely to learn from a dialogue that has some excitement or human interest in it. It is helpful too if the dialogue has some action in it, so that it can be dramatised, not simply said aloud.

4.3.2
Some problems discussed

Although the dialogue is an effective device for contextualising new items of language, especially if it is accompanied, at least in the early stages of the language programme, by a visual sequence that illustrates the main events in the situation, it is unlikely that the students will understand it completely even after they have listened to it two or three times. A good deal of course depends on which new items are being introduced and how many, and how well the context helps to convey their meaning. Without some prior introduction to new language, most students are likely to have only a general idea of what the dialogue is about. While some teachers are satisfied with this on the grounds that meaning is best apprehended in terms of wholes, others think it is wasteful and would prefer their students to have a more complete understanding from the outset. Since, then, this is an area where there is some disagreement, we need to discuss two important problems.

(a) *Should we 'pre-teach' new language in the text?* That is, should we extract items (grammatical or lexical) from the text, teach their meaning (e.g. through translation or in situations and get the learners to practise this language) before we let them listen to the dialogue? The argument in favour of this is that, unless we do some pre-teaching of this kind, the students will not understand the dialogue. The argument against is that the students always end up by understanding; that they should be given the opportunity to guess the meaning of new language and that this in fact is one of the strategies they will need to acquire. It might also be argued that, at least in the early stages, the students will probably be mentally translating the dialogue as they are listening.

It must be acknowledged that there are occasions when it helps to prepare the students for listening by pre-teaching an item which is likely to prevent them from understanding the dialogue as a whole. In practice, however, even near-beginner students accept a global approach which requires them to try to work out the meaning for themselves, especially if they know, because they are familiar with your procedures, that they will be given several opportunities to hear the dialogue; that they can use the visual sequence to help interpret the dialogue; that they will see the text in due course and, finally, that you will explain any difficulties which remain at the end. As a general rule, look at each dialogue on its own merits.

(b) *Should we translate the dialogue, in whole or in part, at any stage of the presentation?* Clearly it should not be necessary to translate the whole of the dialogue, or to get the students to translate it, as a way of making sure that they have understood it. Sometimes it may help to give the mother-tongue equivalent of an item (especially if the alternative is to try to teach its meaning through a procedure, such as demonstration, that would take up a lot of time). This may be necessary when you are clearing up any difficulties after the students have listened to the dialogue several times. Mostly, however, the mother tongue is likely to be needed, particularly in the early stages, to help set the context for the dialogue or to explain certain aspects of the situation, which in itself will help the learners to understand the dialogue better.

Perhaps more important questions which we need to concern ourselves with while working out procedures for presenting dialogues are:

(a) *How do we motivate the students to listen?* Because, unless they listen, they will not learn anything. Ways of doing this are:

(i) through discussion of the situation (together with related visual material) and by relating the situation to the learners themselves (their interests, environment etc.);

(ii) through a pre-listening task which will involve them in the situation/topic on a personal level.

(b) *How can we focus attention on key items in the dialogue?* This can be done through 'focus' questions (which need not always be in the form of questions, of course) which will get the learners to listen out for specific bits of information in the dialogue. A task of this kind also helps to reassure the learners that they are achieving something positive, even if they do not fully understand the dialogue.

(c) *How can we use the dialogue to develop communicative skills?* One important communicative skill that we should seek to develop is listening (and this is one important argument against pre-teaching). There will also be opportunities for talking and exchanging ideas about the situation. Finally, we must see to it that the dialogue leads on to the communicative use of the new language items.

4.3.3
Presenting
dialogues: a basic
approach

The following set of procedures outlines a workable approach to presenting dialogues in average classroom conditions. It need not of course be followed rigidly. Although there are certain things that you will always need to do – such as involving the students in the situation, providing reasons for listening, checking understanding (etc.) – you should look at each dialogue carefully to see what modifications are needed.

The dialogue on page 26 which has been used to illustrate these procedures is taken from a course for adolescent learners and forms part of a loosely-knit story line with recurring characters. The main grammatical item in the dialogue is *can* (to express ability).

Step 1   *Establish the setting* You can do this with the help of the first picture. Point out or get the students to tell you that the boy (Tim, with whom they are familiar) is showing something in a newspaper to his friends. There is going to be a carnival, with a talent competition and a prize of £100. Explain or translate any of these items as necessary. The important thing then is to bring

A

1

TIM: Hey! Look at this. A talent competition!

TINA: Where?

TIM: Here. In the park. At the Carnival.

TONY: The Carnival? What carnival?

TINA: Greenhill Carnival. It's on May the first.

TIM: And there are prizes, too. Look.

TONY: 'First Prize, £100.' Not bad!

2

TINA: What about your song, Tony? It's a good song. Sing it at the Carnival.

TONY: Good idea!

TIM: Tina can sing it with you. She's a good singer.

TONY: What about you, Tim? Can you sing?

TINA: No. Tim can't sing.

3

TONY: Can you play the guitar, Tim?

TIM: Yes, I can. Listen to this.

4

TIM: It's a good little guitar. Whose is it? Ringo's?

TONY: No. Ringo can't play the guitar.

TINA: But he can play the drums. Listen! He's clever, isn't he?

From M Palmer and D Byrne *Track* Students' Book 1 (Longman 1982) these ideas alive for the students e.g. by asking them what they know about carnivals (especially any famous ones), whether they have ever taken part in one (or in a talent competition) and whether they would like to. You may have to use the mother tongue quite a lot at this point, but use English as much as possible because discussing topics like this often provides opportunities for exposing the learners to a good deal of informal language.

Step 2   *Establish a personal link with the situation*   Elicit and list on the board some of the things you can do at a carnival. For example, you can sing, dance, play the guitar (and other musical instruments). This provides a way, in this case, of introducing *can* informally because you need it for an activity (so that in effect you are doing *some* pre-teaching). Ask the students to interview one another quickly about what things they can do. (This activity can be done in greater depth at the practice stage, bringing in more vocabulary.) You could also tell the students that there is going to be a class talent competition and get them to say what they can do.

Step 3   *Pre-teach selected items (optional)*   Deal with any difficulties that might seriously interfere with overall understanding and enjoyment of the dialogue. Any such items in this dialogue have already been dealt with incidentally.

Step 4   *Set a listening task*   Since singing is a key activity in the dialogue, a possible task is to ask the students to find out while they are listening who can sing, or who is going to sing at the carnival. The task can be presented in the form of a chart like the one below, that has to be completed with *yes* or *no*.

	sing
Tony	
Tim	
Tina	

Step 5   *Ask the students to listen*   While they are doing this, they may follow the picture sequence but not look at the text. Let them listen to the dialogue as often as they like, and ask for the answers to the focus questions at any suitable point. You can also ask other questions to see how much the students have understood so far. (They may also like to ask *you* questions!)

Step 6   *Ask the students to read silently as they listen*   During this phase, pause after each section and ask some simple questions to check understanding. For example (after Section 1): *Where is the talent competition? Is the Carnival today? Are there any prizes? What is the first prize?* (etc.)

Step 7   *Ask the students to listen and repeat*   Ask the students to listen again (without looking at the text) and to repeat selected utterances either in chorus or individually. Note that most learners enjoy repeating in chorus. Your task is to see that it is effective (see 5.1.1).

Step 8   *Explain any difficulties*   You can do this by reading through the dialogue, drawing attention to any points (perhaps giving further examples of an item) or by asking the students to tell you what difficulties they have.

Step 9   *Ask the students to practise saying the dialogue*   Divide the learners into small groups for this. They should decide among themselves who will take which part. Carry out selective checking, but get the learners themselves to listen to and correct one another.

Step 10   Get the students to dramatise or improvise the dialogue. One or two groups can be asked to do this if there is time and if they want to.

4.4
Presenting
prose passages

Dialogues, as we noted in 4.2, provide not only samples of spoken language which the learners need in order to build up their oral ability, but also a framework for using them: they show the learners how speakers interact. However, in order to talk, we need something to talk about – a topic of some kind – and dialogues in coursebooks, especially in the early stages of a course, rarely provide an actual stimulus for talk. Passages, on the other hand, whether they tell a story, describe places or events or are informative in other ways, offer plenty of content. For this reason, provided that the learners are acquiring sufficient conversational forms through dialogues and other oral activities, passages are likely to provide a healthy addition to an otherwise insipid diet. It is likely too that the learners will find them more attractive, especially if they feel that they are actually *learning something* in addition to new language.

4.4.1
Some problems
discussed

Passages are, however, more difficult to handle as presentation texts, especially in the early stages. The language may be complex (more typical of the written form of the language) and topics may require the introduction of more vocabulary. Ideas in the text may present the students with problems of comprehension. There is obviously a risk here of returning to traditional procedures, with the teacher reading the text aloud, explaining and then questioning the students. This will not be an effective way of developing oral skills.

Should we, then, follow the same approach as for presenting dialogues? Certainly we do not *have* to. In the first place, if we do decide to ask the students to listen to the passage before they read it, on the grounds that they need to listen to different kinds of texts (not just dialogues), we could lighten the load by doing selective pre-teaching. Alternatively, we can adopt a reading-oriented approach from the start, concentrating on getting the students to learn through reading, and then using the texts for various kinds

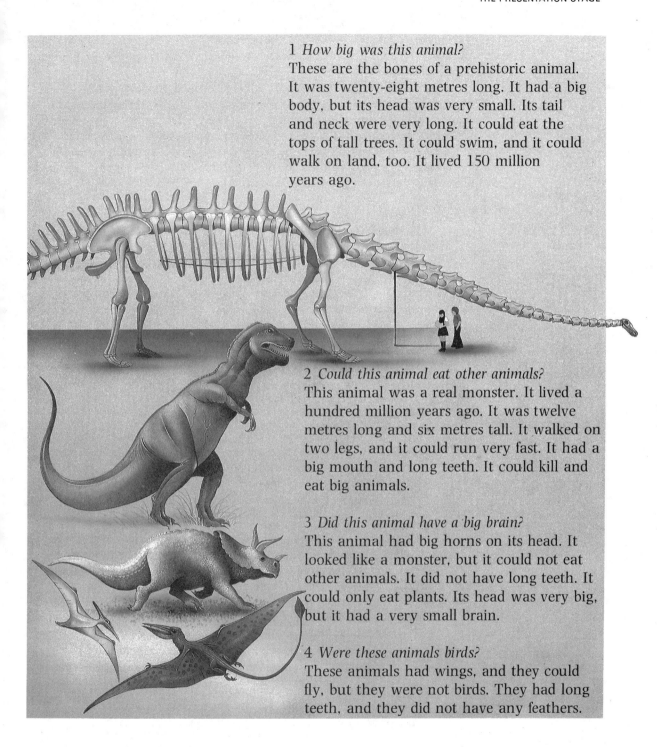

1 *How big was this animal?*
These are the bones of a prehistoric animal. It was twenty-eight metres long. It had a big body, but its head was very small. Its tail and neck were very long. It could eat the tops of tall trees. It could swim, and it could walk on land, too. It lived 150 million years ago.

2 *Could this animal eat other animals?*
This animal was a real monster. It lived a hundred million years ago. It was twelve metres long and six metres tall. It walked on two legs, and it could run very fast. It had a big mouth and long teeth. It could kill and eat big animals.

3 *Did this animal have a big brain?*
This animal had big horns on its head. It looked like a monster, but it could not eat other animals. It did not have long teeth. It could only eat plants. Its head was very big, but it had a very small brain.

4 *Were these animals birds?*
These animals had wings, and they could fly, but they were not birds. They had long teeth, and they did not have any feathers.

From M Palmer and D Byrne *Track* Students' Book 1 (Longman 1982) of related oral practice, especially discussion of ideas in the passage. In the end, our students will probably benefit equally from either approach, although in different ways.

Again, therefore, a flexible approach is advocated, looking at each text to see how it is best presented. You could follow, broadly, the procedures outlined for presenting dialogues in 4.3.3. However, for the text on page 29, which contains not only a good deal of new language but also a lot of information which will probably be new to the students, a reading-oriented approach is suggested. You will probably find this effective for many passages of this kind where there is a good deal of new information.

4.4.2
Presenting prose
passages: a basic
approach

Step 1   *Introduce the topic*   Refer to the pictures, for example, to get the students to tell you something about prehistoric monsters. Ask them about books they have read, films or TV programmes they have seen. Much of this will probably have to be done in the mother tongue. But then ask them to tell you in English some of the things they know about prehistoric monsters and write these on one side of the board.

> *PREHISTORIC MONSTERS*
> *We know:*
> *– they were very big*
> *– they lived a long time ago*

Step 2   *Introduce the text*   Read the first paragraph with the class and explain (or translate) key language items e.g. *could* (if necessary), parts of the body and measurement (... *metres long*). Probably very little explanation will be needed, but at least working through the first part of the passage with the students helps to reassure them.

Step 3   *Provide relevant language practice*   For example, get the students to tell you (or ask for) parts of the body which they can see in the pictures. At this stage they will not actually know which ones will occur in the text. Play a word game (e.g. Word Bingo) to involve them in remembering the words. You can practise measurement by guessing and then measuring the lengths of items in the classroom. Practice along these lines provides some relaxed pre-teaching of relevant items. The students may end up learning and using more than they actually need for the text.

Step 4   *Set a reading task*   For example, you could use the questions at the head of each section. An alternative task, for which the questions do not relate to any specific section, could be:

> *Which of these animals could* | *fly?*
> *run fast?*
> *eat other animals?*
> *swim?*

Step 5   *Do silent reading*   Ask the students to read the passage silently and find the answers to the reading task.

Step 6   *Read the passage aloud*   While you are doing this, ask for the answers to the reading task. Ask other simple questions to check understanding.

Step 7   *Explain any difficulties*   Ask the students what difficulties they still have. Encourage them to guess the meaning of words as much as possible.

Step 8   *Do silent reading*   Tell the class that this will be followed by an activity (e.g. one of those in Step 9).

Step 9   *Get the class to talk about what they have learned*   While this will involve using new language, the emphasis will be on making the students aware that they have learned something through English too. Two possible activities are suggested below. It is acknowledged that in a way we are already moving into the practice stage through these activities.

(a) *Group quizzes*   Divide the class into groups. Ask each to work out quizzes (3–5 questions) for another group. Preparation of the quizzes will involve both talking and writing. The groups then exchange quizzes. Books should be closed while these are being answered. Again this will involve talking and writing. The quizzes are then passed back for correction.

(b) *Class competition* (books closed)   Remember that we started by getting the class to say what they already knew about prehistoric monsters. This information was written on one side of the board. Now divide the rest of the board into four sections, one for each group.

PREHISTORIC MONSTERS We know: – they were very big – they lived a long time ago	GROUP A	GROUP B 2 cd walk on two legs
	GROUP C	GROUP D 3 had small brain

Then ask each group in turn to tell you something new that they have learnt from the passage. E.g. *The second animal could walk on two legs. The third animal had a very small brain.* If there is space, write these ideas on the board, in the appropriate section for each group. This can be done in note form, as shown in the model. The important thing about this activity is to show the learners *how much they have learned* from reading – and that they can *talk about it*, too!

4.5
Alternative procedures at the presentation stage

It is convenient to look at these under two headings:

(a) *structured activities*: these are designed to give the learners a systematic introduction to an item of language in order to make its meaning clear.

(b) *unstructured activities*: the main purpose of these is to get the learners to communicate with the language they already know in order to decide what new language they need to be taught (see 1.2.4).

4.5.1
Structured activities

Most structured activities form part of the repertoire of traditional language teaching. For example, you can use classroom contexts or create situations in the classroom, particularly through the use of realia, actions or visual material, to illustrate the meaning of new items. To present *can* (to express ability), which was the main item in the dialogue in 4.3, you can first of all talk to the class about the things that you can do: e.g. *I can swim. I can play the guitar, but I can't play the piano* (etc.). You can accompany these examples with mime or appropriate visual material to help make the meaning clear, and you can translate the item if this proves really necessary (as with presentation through texts, the general intention of this approach is that the learners should work out the meanings for themselves). The learners are then asked to talk about themselves in the same way. Similarly, to present *there is/are* (+ adverbial phrases of place), you can provide a context by drawing a picture, using a wallchart or creating a scene on the magnetboard. At a more advanced level, the presentation of items is likely to be more abstract: for example, an anecdote or story in which the new language forms a part or emerges as the conclusion: e.g. *I was out for a walk the other day. Suddenly it began to rain hard. I hadn't got a raincoat with me, but luckily I had a large sheet of plastic in my bag, so I put it over my head. If I hadn't had this with me, I would have got wet ... and I might have caught cold!*

It could of course be objected that such techniques of presentation are, on the whole, not 'communicative' since in many cases students can see for themselves what we are telling them about. For example, if we show them a picture of a park and tell them that there are trees in the park, leaves on the trees (etc.), we are in effect talking about the obvious. However, this is not necessarily how the learners, anxious to learn new language, will view it. More important is whether they learn effectively and whether they are motivated to learn in this way. Generally, therefore, although a global approach in which the learners are exposed to new language in 'chunks', through texts of various kinds, is to be preferred (and in any case is likely to be the one used in the coursebook), these techniques should be accepted as a quick, effective way of conveying the meaning of items. The *real* learning of these items, however, will probably depend more on the opportunities which the learners are given to use them at the practice stage. Structured presentation techniques are, of course, useful for some quick pre-teaching (see 4.3.2) or to elucidate a point in a text which the context has failed to make clear.

4.5.2
Unstructured activities

These are clearly more suitable at the post-elementary level, where the learners know enough of the language to 'have a go' at communicating. You can therefore use almost any of the activities in Chapters 8–10 as a way of finding out what items of language you need to teach the learners in order to improve their ability to communicate. If the learners are working in groups, this means that you must monitor the activities very carefully to determine which items there is a common need for. Alternatively, some activities with the class as a whole will generally show up the areas where new language has to be taught.

However, even at a fairly elementary level this approach can be used from time to time. For example, if you are using the picture of the room on page 62 (without the numbered positions), the learners can be asked to decide where they would like to locate a number of objects (e.g. a lamp, a clock, a vase of flowers etc.). If you are working with the class as a whole, you can invite suggestions which will soon result in the learners reaching the limits of their language. For example, if they know *in*, *on* and *under* (which might be regarded as a basic prepositional kit!), they will want to know how to express *near*, *in front of*, *behind* (etc.).

Clearly, however, such an approach is difficult to implement consistently unless it is built into the structure of the coursebook (or unless you are free to determine the scope and direction of your teaching, which is often possible only at the advanced level). There is little point in getting the learners to determine for you what language could best be taught next if the coursebook proceeds in a different direction! Unstructured activities as a way of identifying learners' needs at the presentation stage are, on the whole, best used as a supplementary procedure particularly in areas where you might like to anticipate or expand the teaching of items in the coursebook. It is a particularly effective way of making the learners aware of what new vocabulary they need and as such can often be used to supplement the sometimes meagre amount of vocabulary in the coursebook.

Discussion	1 Do you agree that both dialogues and prose texts can be equally effective, in their different ways, in developing oral skills? If you would prefer to use only dialogues in the early stages, give your reasons.
	2 To what extent do you think translation, as a way of conveying meaning, should be used when presenting new language? What are some of the advantages and disadvantages?
	3 Do you think that it is essential to use texts as the main way of presenting new language? What are the advantages and disadvantages?
Exercises	1 Examine any coursebook to see what kind of texts are used to present new language.
	2 Use the criteria in 4.3.1 to evaluate one of the dialogues in the coursebook.
	3 Select a dialogue from the coursebook and show how you would present it following the basic approach in 4.3.3.
References	1 On the presentation stage, see: J Willis (1981) Ch 14; R Scott in K Johnson and K Morrow (eds.) (1981); J Harmer (1983) Ch 6; P Hubbard et al (1983) pp 3–15; S Holden (ed.) (1983b) 1.2 and 1.3; A Matthews et al (eds.) (1985) Ch 2.
	2 For specific guidance on presenting dialogues and prose texts, see D Byrne and M Palmer: *Track* Introduction to Teacher's Book 1 (Longman 1982).

5

The Practice stage (1): The use of drills

5.1
The needs of the learners

After new items have been presented in meaningful contexts, and some imitation and repetition been carried out, the students must be given ample opportunity to practise these items for themselves. That is to say, they need:

(a) *practice* They must be allowed to *use* the items. There is no substitute for this (e.g. translation or explanation).

(b) *oral practice* As far as possible, they should be given practice that does not involve constant reference to a text.

(c) *guided oral practice* This is needed to build up the confidence of the learners to use new items by ensuring that they have something to say and can say it without too much hesitation.

(d) *meaningful oral practice* Because drills are guided, this does not mean that they have to be mechanical. The learners should at all times understand and pay attention to what they are required to say, and their utterances should not only be *correct* (as far as possible: mistakes at this stage should be kept to a minimum because they slow up the lesson) but *appropriate* to the situation. Practice must therefore take place in a context.

(e) *extensive oral practice* Your task at this stage is to see that the learners get sufficient practice, not to do the talking yourself.

Does the solution, especially with large classes, lie partly or mainly in some form of choral practice? This technique is discussed first, since it is commonly used in many classrooms.

5.1.1
Chorus work

As its name implies, this technique requires a number of students to speak in unison. You can ask the whole class to do this at the same time if it is not too large, or you can divide the class up into smaller units. For example:

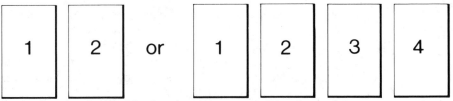

Each choral unit should relate in some way to how the students are already arranged in rows.

The following procedures for choral work are suggested:

(a) *Provide a clear model.* The students cannot be expected to imitate what they cannot hear.

(b) *Select the material for choral repetition carefully.* Some sentences in a text may not be suitable for repetition because they are too long.

(c) *Control the choral responses.* Use, for example, a gesture to tell the class when to begin to repeat a sentence after you, and also to indicate the rhythm (i.e. the words or syllables that are stressed).

(d) *Listen out for mistakes.* One way of ensuring that you can hear what the students are saying is to build up the chorus gradually (using what is known as the 'ripple' technique). Ask one student to speak; then with a circular movement of your hand include two or three more, and then expand the chorus by bringing in still more. By building up the chorus step by step, you are better able to hear what is being said on each occasion, and thus able to detect mistakes. The students too are kept more alert since they do not know at what point they will be called upon to speak.

(e) *Correct mistakes* If the students have difficulty in repeating a sentence correctly, there are two key ways in which you can help them to build it up step by step:

Back chaining For this you start at the end of the sentence.

tonight?

going tonight?

are you going tonight?

Where are you going tonight?

Front chaining For this you start at the beginning of the sentence.
I'm
I'm going
I'm going to the
I'm going to the cinema.

When should we use chorus work? At the presentation stage, it is convenient to get the students to repeat parts of the dialogue in this way. It gives them some practice in speaking, if only through imitation, and they often get some reassurance from being allowed to speak in chorus before they are asked to say something as individuals. Provided you move around among the students and listen carefully, you can usually detect the grosser errors. At the practice stage too some repetition, especially of model sentences, will be

35

required. But what other forms of practice can be done through chorus work? The answer seems to be *drills*: controlled practice which permits the students to perform only in a fixed way. Chorus work, then, seems to be a natural associate of the mechanical drills discussed in 5.3. If these are an effective way of giving oral practice, it will be logical to use choral techniques for doing this on an extensive scale.

5.2
Reading aloud as a practice technique

Since reading aloud is still widely used in many classrooms as a practice technique, we must look briefly at what it achieves. First, it does not help students to read more efficiently because normally reading is silent reading. Secondly, it is not an effective way of improving pronunciation. It is true that getting students to read aloud is one way of finding out whether they can pronounce written forms (words, sentences or longer units) and we may sometimes want to do this, especially in the early stages. However, if we want to improve pronunciation, this is normally best done without reference to a written text (and in fact many of the activities in this chapter will also help to improve the students' pronunciation). Finally, one serious objection to getting students to read aloud on any scale is that it takes up (and in many cases wastes) a lot of class time. The one person who may be actually deriving some small benefit from it (i.e. by improving his skill to read aloud) is the student who is reading aloud; the rest of the class are probably not listening with any interest.

There will be a few occasions when the students can be profitably asked to read aloud. For example, we have already noted (4.3.3) that they can be asked to read the dialogue aloud in small groups, and this can be done for other activities too. Also it should be kept in mind that if you really want the students to pay attention to someone reading aloud, make sure that they are actually listening and hearing something new. For example, when students have done a group activity which involves making a report to the whole class, they can be asked to read this aloud. Students will pay attention because they are learning something new, while the person reading aloud must do it well otherwise he will not be able to convey his message. This clearly is not the case when students are merely reading aloud a text which everyone is familiar with. For this and other reasons, then, reading aloud in general is not a useful practice technique.

5.3
Mechanical drills

It may seem superfluous to describe drills as mechanical. Surely that is what all drills are: a form of linguistic discipline, requiring the learners to *perform correctly* regardless of whether they have to *think* about what they are saying? Certainly the students can get *extensive* practice in this way, and generally they can speak without too much intervention on the part of the teacher. This is one of the attractions of drills: they increase the amount of student talking time. The learners can produce almost effortlessly an endless stream of *correct* sentences, and this must be attractive if you have a large number of students in your class. And of course this kind of language activity is at least *one* step forward from mere imitation, and less discouraging than getting responses that are full of mistakes.

The extensive use of mechanical drills, particularly the kind discussed below, derives largely from an approach to language learning which has been mostly superseded – one that placed great emphasis on the formation of correct habits and the avoidance of mistakes. However, it would perhaps be wrong to assume that the students gain nothing from some forms of practice that try to exclude all possibility of error. For one thing, they gain some confidence and fluency at the level of pronunciation and also in those areas of the language system (noun and verb inflections, concord etc.) which require a good deal of practice. But it is extremely doubtful whether mechanical procedures (such as substitution activities below) have any learning value beyond this: it is a common experience for students to *repeat* dozens of sentences of a certain type and yet be unable to *produce* the same type of sentence for themselves. These procedures seem to leave the learners where they started off: at the level of repetition.

5.3.1
Substitution drills

The substitution table, as shown in the table below, is the most condensed form of this type of drill.

There	is	a	river café dog	in the park.
	are	some	trees flowers children	

The material to be practised is presented to the students in written form (e.g. perhaps written up on the board). Only correct sentences can be formed from the table provided that the learners follow the conventions that separate singular from plural forms. The table could in fact have been made more challenging by mixing up the singular and plural nouns in the fourth column.

The same pattern could be practised through an oral substitution drill, using callwords as prompts (i.e. to elicit the sentences the students have to say).

T: There is a river in the park.
ss: There is a river in the park.
T: Dog.
ss: There is a dog in the park (etc.).

Both types of practice, however, are completely mechanical. Could anything be done to make them less so? With the substitution table, if we accept that an important goal of this kind of activity is not only the *practice* of correct language but also the *understanding* of how grammar works, we could make much more effective use of tables like these. For example:

(a) We can ask the students to make *true* sentences i.e. by reference to a text they have read or heard or a picture of some kind.

(b) We can ask the students to complete the table i.e. again by reference to a text or picture. In this case we might leave the students to supply all the nouns.

(c) We could ask the students to make up their own tables from jumbled words e.g.

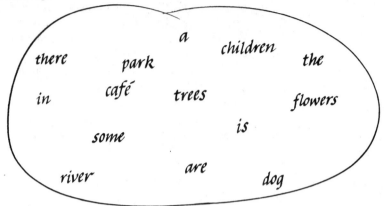

there
in
park
café
a
trees
children
is
the
flowers
some
river
are
dog

For the oral drill, the substitution of nouns in the fourth slot could be cued by picture cards, as an alternative to actually providing the learners with the words.

However, although in this way the learners have to pay more attention to the form of what they are saying, the drill still remains inherently mechanical. The learners do not have to pay any real attention to *meaning*.

5.3.2 Transformation (or Conversion) drills

Transformation drills are used to practise changes, for example, from affirmative to interrogative or negative; from one pronoun form to another, and from active to passive (etc.). The teacher starts with a model sentence:

T: I get up early every morning. Use TOM.
A: Tom gets up early every morning.
T: I have a bath.
B: He has a bath.
T: I have breakfast at about seven-thirty.
C: He has breakfast at about seven-thirty (*etc.*).

Although the structural areas for which this type of drill is commonly used undoubtedly require a great deal of practice, it is unlikely that the students will master them in this way. There are, clearly, alternative ways of practising these structural items: for example, by using picture strips. The sentences can then be elicited without recourse to transformation.

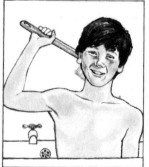

There are, however, certain situations in real life in which we do actually transform or convert what people say: for example, when we report what someone has said. One way, then, of making such practice more meaningful is by getting the students to 'report' the utterances to one another. For example:

T: I'm going to a party this evening.
A *(to B)*: Did you hear that? He's going to a party!
T: I'm going to buy a new shirt for the party.
B *(to C)*: Just imagine! He's going to buy a new shirt!

At a later stage many aspects of indirect speech can be realistically practised in this way. Chain reporting (i.e. one student speaking to another round or across the class) adds to the interest. But drills of this kind proceed of course at a much slower pace.

**5.3.3
Conclusion**

There are many more types of mechanical drill. Indeed they are a common feature of many textbooks. Question and answer practice is often carried out quite mechanically, as, for example, when students are required to reply to questions such as *Did you (stay at home last night?/watch TV?/go to bed early? etc.)* using a fixed type of response (e.g. *Yes, I did*). Conditioned responses to questions are a degree worse than the drills above (we normally ask questions in order to find something out). But if we left the drill open (*Answer these questions honestly!*) the sequence would no longer be predictable. If the student replies 'no' to the first question, the rest of the drill collapses. In this case we can no longer focus his attention on a particular type of response, as above. But it is much more likely that we shall succeed in getting him to pay attention to the *meaning* of what he is saying.

**5.4
Meaningful
practice**

We have seen that mechanical drills can provide *extensive* practice – because most of them can be done in chorus, and *rapid* practice – because once the students have understood the form of the drill, they can be prompted to continue with just a single cue. But they are not meaningful. It looks, then, as if there is a conflict between the various needs of the learners at this stage, and perhaps this conflict cannot be fully resolved so long as the class is taught as a single unit (see 7.1). But since at this stage you will often want to teach the whole class together, let us first of all concentrate on ways of making practice more meaningful, regardless of whether it sometimes goes at a rather slower pace. To some extent we may have to be slightly less concerned about the students always making correct responses. The classroom is a more flexible place than the language laboratory (which at one time encouraged the use of mechanical drills): drills can be modified, alternative responses can be asked for and, if necessary, mistakes corrected.

**5.4.1
Guessing drills**

One of the simplest and most effective ways of giving rapid whole class practice is to get the learners to try to find something out through guessing. By doing this we are in effect setting up a simple 'information gap' situation (see 9.1), which is the basis of a good many communicative activities, especially games, because the learners are trying to find out something that they do not know.

Some examples are given below:

(a) The students think of their favourite colour (sport, hobby, animal etc.). They then take it in turns to find out about each other's colours (etc.) by asking: *Is it (red)?* (etc.)

(b) The students are told they are going to emigrate and they have to decide which country they are going to live in. They then take turns to find out the name of each other's country by asking: *Are you going to live in (China)?* (etc.) The pattern used here can of course be varied: *Is it ...?/Would you like to ...?/Have you decided to ...?*

(c) The students think or make up something that they did the previous evening (or weekend or on their last holiday). They then take turns to find out what it is by asking: *Did you go (swimming)?* (etc.)

(d) The students have to imagine that they have been ill. They then take turns to find out each other's illness by asking: *Have you had* (or: *Did you have*) *(pneumonia)?* (etc.)

(e) The students have to pretend that they are old and to choose an occupation that they would have liked to have when they were young. They then take turns to find out each other's occupation by asking: *Would you have liked to be (an engineer)?* (etc.)

It should be clear that this is a very effective device for practising a wide range of structural items (tenses, modal forms, patterns etc.) and vocabulary items i.e. lexical sets such as months of the year, food, clothes etc.), all of which not only require a good deal of immediate practice when they are first presented but also need constant revision. If there are a lot of items in the lexical set to be practised, write a list on the board, with the help of suggestions from the class, who can be asked to spell some of the words for you. This means that the students will be guessing from a limited range of choices and this makes the activity go more smoothly.

You should also note that the structural level of the questions can be scaled up or down according to the level and needs of the class. For example, occupations can be practised within the framework of *Are you ...?/Are you going to be ...?/Would you like to be ...?* (etc.) All you need to do is to invent a situation into which the appropriate pattern can be fitted. Also, although the activity may encourage the use of interrogative forms (which of course need a lot of practice), the students can also find out the answer by asking: *You're a doctor, aren't you? I think you're a teacher. Perhaps you're a (journalist).* If you want to practise the third person singular forms *he/she*, two students can work together and confide in one another, so that the students who are trying to find out have to ask: *Does (he) want to be a (bus driver)?*

Some points to keep in mind when doing this activity are:

(a) Start off by getting the students to try to find out something about you. This provides an opportunity to give a variety of *responses* (e.g. *Well, no/No, of course not/Well, not exactly/No, I'm afraid not.* etc.) Then, when the class are trying to find out about one of themselves, join in the questioning so as to suggest different ways of trying to find out the answer.

(b) It is a good idea to get the students to write down what they have decided (e.g. their favourite colour). Sometimes they forget what they have decided in the excitement of the game. The students can also be given picture or word cards, although this of course does not allow them any personal choice.

(c) Don't insist on the students repeating the complete pattern every time (e.g. *Would you have liked to be a (doctor)?*). As they get more and more involved in trying to find out the answer, they will naturally take short cuts and ask: *A (doctor)?* You can re-introduce the pattern from time to time.

The same technique can be used with visual material. Pictures, for example, are often used to contextualise language drills, particularly in the form of question and answer practice, but since the students can actually *see* what they are talking about, there is no 'information gap'. However, if the students have *not* seen the picture, but have been given some idea of what it is about (for example, for the picture below, you might say: *It's a picture of a room. There are some people in* it. How much information you give will depend on the activity), they can then ask real questions (i.e. requests for information) such as: *Is there (a TV) in the room? Is there (a clock) (on the bookcase)?* (etc.). It is assumed that for drill-like practice at this stage you will probably want to focus on a single pattern.

For this type of work small pictures (e.g. cutouts from magazines, photos) are suitable because they only have to be visible to the person – you or one of the students – who is answering the questions and, of course, are easier to keep hidden from the rest of the class. Practice does not have to be

41

restricted to questions. The students can, for example, make assertions (e.g. *I think there's a vase of flowers on the bookcase*), which those who can see the picture accept or reject (e.g. *Yes, you're quite right. There is* or: *Sorry, you're wrong. There isn't*).

5.4.2
Imaginary
situations

This activity is similar to the previous one in that it involves an 'information gap'. The imaginary situation is sketched in. For example: *I've just bought a house. I haven't much money and I'm furnishing it very slowly.* The students are then asked to form questions of their own using a particular pattern (e.g. the Present Perfect with *yet* would be suitable for the situation above).

T: Now I want you to ask me questions. For example: Have you bought a table yet?
A: Have you bought a bed yet?
T: Yes, of course I've bought a bed.
B: Have you bought a TV set yet?
T: No, I haven't.
C: Have you bought a fridge yet?
T: Yes, I've just bought one.

The same situation could be used to practise question tags. For example, in this case the students make assertions such as: *I suppose you've bought some chairs, haven't you?* Or: *I imagine you haven't bought any pictures yet, have you?*

Some situations can be set up with just a single sentence, as in the drill below, which practises Conditional sentences of the type *If + Simple Present/modal verb*.

T: I hear that George wants to have a meeting tomorrow. If he rings *me*, I'll say I'm busy. Now make *your* excuses.
A: If he asks *me*, I'll say I'm not free.
B: If he rings *me*, I'll say I'm not well.
C: If he asks *me*, I'll say it's too soon *(etc.)*.

In the last drill of this kind which we shall look at, the students' responses are in fact completely controlled. Its meaning for them lies not so much in *what* they say but in *how* they say it, and in the fact that they talk to one another. In each case the situation involves gossiping about another person.

T: Listen.   Mary eats a lot.
          She eats too much!
          I wish she wouldn't eat so much!
(The students repeat these sentences until they can say them with correct stress and intonation.)

T: JOHN – DRINK *(indicates three students to speak)*
A: John drinks a lot.
B: He drinks too much!
C: I wish he wouldn't drink so much!
T: ANN – SMOKE *(indicates three students to speak)*

A: Ann smokes a lot.
B: She smokes too much!
C: I wish she wouldn't smoke so much! *(etc.)*.

5.4.3
Open-ended responses

Many patterns can be practised by giving only part of a sentence or a clause and letting the students suggest various ways of completing it. Although this type of practice is not contextualised, the students are required to give answers which are both *correct* and *appropriate*. The drill below practises *have* as an action verb.

T: John was hungry, so he had a sandwich.
   Now suggest other possibilities.
A: ..., so perhaps he had some biscuits.
B: ..., so maybe he had some bread and cheese.
C: ..., so he had some chocolate.
T: Mary was thirsty ...
A: ..., so maybe she had a cup of tea.
B: ..., so perhaps she had a glass of water.
C: ..., so she had a glass of beer.
T: Tom was dirty, ...
A: ..., so perhaps he had a bath.
B: ..., so maybe he had a shower.
C: ..., so he had a wash *(etc.)*.

5.4.4
Practising concepts

We noted in 4.3.1. (a) that the key items in the dialogue should be especially those needed to express such concepts as obligation, approval and disapproval, agreement and disagreement, advice, warnings etc. Clearly a great deal of guided practice will be needed in these areas to reinforce what the students have been exposed to through the dialogue. Such practice could easily become mechanical: it must therefore be combined with procedures already indicated (e.g. the appropriate use of visual aids and imaginary situations). In the drill below, for example, contradictions are practised with reference to the picture in 5.4.1.

T: John's reading a book.
A: No, he isn't. He's watching television.
T: Mary's watching television.
B: No, she isn't. She's doing her homework.
T: Their mother's sweeping the floor.
C: No, she isn't. She's looking out of the window *(etc)*.

It should be noticed that the drill in fact practises a single tense form (the Present Continuous) but what makes it meaningful for the students is the framework of assertion and contradiction. There is also no reason why such drills should not be further livened up by teaching the students to use such expressions as *Don't be silly!* or *Don't talk nonsense!*

In the next drill, suggestions (with *Let's ...,*) and objections (with *But we haven't got ...*) are practised.

T: Let's make some sandwiches.
A: But we haven't got any butter!
B: But we haven't got any cheese!
C: But we haven't got any bread!
T: Let's make a salad, then.
A: But we haven't got any lettuce!
B: But we haven't got any tomatoes!
C: But we haven't got any oil. *(etc.).*

Again, the *situation* must be set up before the drill is begun. A pictorial aid would also be useful: for example, a chart showing different foods, from which the students can select appropriate items. An important thing to notice about these drills is that they can be done at different levels. For example, the suggestion might take the form: *Why don't we ...?* and the objection: *Well, we can't, can we? We've run out of ...*

Various responses are possible in the drill below, which practises intention (*I'm going to ...*) and objection *(But you can't ..., can you?).* The drill also practises relationships between verb and noun (e.g. drive – car/ride – bike etc.) The items referred to are those illustrated in the picture set.

T: I'm going to buy a car.
A: But you can't drive, can you?
T: BIKE
B: I'm going to buy a bike.
C: But you can't ride, can you?
   Point to two more students, who choose their own items.
D: I'm going to buy a piano.
E: But you can't play, can you? (*etc.*)

Alternative responses, at different levels of difficulty, would be: *But do you know how to play?/You <u>do</u> know how to play, don't you?/I didn't know you knew how to play./I didn't know you could play.*

5.4.5
Expressing
relationships

An effective way of making the students think about what they are saying in a drill is to focus their attention on the meaning relationships that exist between different elements such as sentences, clauses, phrases and words. In the drill below, for example, the students are invited to *draw inferences* from statements made by the teacher. (The drill also practises *must* to express strong probability.)

T: I've been working *all* day.
A: You must be tired!
T: I haven't eaten a thing since breakfast.
B: You must be hungry!
T: I haven't had anything to drink either.
C: You must be thirsty!
T: And now I'm going to a party.
D: You must be . . . mad!

In the drill above, the students state *consequences* (except in the last example). In the drill below, they suggest *reasons*.

T: I just couldn't lift the box.
A: I suppose it was too heavy.
T: I couldn't get anything to eat in the cafe.
B: I suppose you were too late.
C: Perhaps you were too early.
T: I feel very tired today.
D: Perhaps you didn't go to bed early enough last night (*etc.*).

Perhaps the chief value of this type of practice is that it can be used to develop the students' awareness of underlying grammatical relationships by getting them to perform such operations as *definition* (*What's (an artist)? Oh, he's a man who (paints pictures)*) and *paraphrase*, as in the drill below.

T: The box was so heavy I just couldn't lift it.
A: Oh, it was too heavy for you to lift, was it?
T: The questions were so difficult I just couldn't answer them.
B: Oh, they were too difficult for you to answer, were they?

5.4.6
Conclusions

There is clearly more than one way of making practice meaningful for the students. Although these have been discussed under different headings, it is possible to combine these procedures to great effect. For example, concepts can – and generally should – be practised in conjunction with pictorial aids. However, in the absence of a context, it is very easy to revert to mechanical practice. This is true of the last example in 5.4.5. For, although it is true to life in the sense that we do often paraphrase, by way of comment, what somebody says to us, it is in fact little more than a variant of the transformation drill discussed in 5.3.2. Clearly, then, you have to be constantly on the lookout to ensure that the procedure you have chosen does in fact make practice meaningful.

One final factor that must not be overlooked in this discussion of drills is that of enjoyment. Students can easily become bored with repetition, especially if this involves mindless repetition. If, however, we can introduce an element of fun – through whatever means: competition, invention or trying to find something out – the drill becomes more like a kind of game and what is being practised is more likely to be memorable. This question is further discussed in Chapter 9.

Discussion

1 What is your opinion of the following techniques?
   (a) reading aloud; (b) chorus work; (c) mechanical drills.
2 How would you try to keep mistakes to a minimum at the practice stage?
3 What steps would you take to see that repetition through drill-like activities is memorable?

Exercises

1 Examine any textbook to see what kind of drills are used or recommended. If mechanical drills are used, could you make them more meaningful?
2 Give other examples of language items (structures, functions or vocabulary) that could be practised through guessing drills.
3 Give examples of any drills which you have found effective at the practice stage.

References

1 On controlled practice, see:
   – J Harmer (1983) 7.1;
   – J Willis (1981) Ch 15.
2 On the practice stage in general, see:
   – H Moorwood (ed.) (1978) Section 2;
   – G Abbott and P Wingard (1981) Ch 5;
   – E Stevick (1982) Chs 8–10;
   – A Matthews et al (eds.) (1985) Ch 3.

6

The Practice stage (2): The use of texts

6.1
The text as a context for language practice

Now that we have looked at other ways of giving guided oral practice at the practice stage, we are in a better position to appreciate both the advantages and disadvantages of exploiting texts (dialogues and prose passages) for this purpose.

First, however, we need to be clear about one issue. Most coursebooks include a section of activities based on a presentation text, often under the heading of *Comprehension*. These are mostly in the form of questions on the text, true/false statements, completion exercises (etc.). If these are truly intended to test comprehension of the text, then we should not be using them for oral practice of the kind we have in mind at this stage. We can of course discuss the answers with the students when they have done the exercises (i.e. as homework, individually or as pairwork in class), but we should not expect the students to come up with the answers either quickly (because this will not encourage them to read the text) or from memory. On the other hand, 'comprehension' questions are often disguised language practice activities: that is, they are intended to give the students an opportunity to say or write something rather than to develop reading skills.

For the moment we will assume that the exercises on the presentation text are intended for this purpose. Their advantage, over some of the drills we have looked at, is that they offer a very well-defined context for practice. On the other hand, the text is not so immediately accessible as a wallchart or an 'imaginary situation'. It is a sequence of sentences, printed on a page or recorded on tape, which the students have only partially in their memories. Clearly we cannot give effective oral practice if the students have to keep referring to their books, but at the same time we want to avoid putting a strain on their memories.

There is no single solution to this problem. Sometimes the answer is to let the students work in pairs first, doing the exercise on their own (in which case we have to relax our control of the activity) before going over the answers with the class as a whole. This approach is to be recommended mainly because it is more learner-centred: it gives all the students an opportunity to talk while working out the answers. However, if you do want to do some whole class practice based on the text, you must either make sure that the students are totally familiar with the text (i.e. through re-reading) or break the text down into small chunks so that you can focus on one section at a time.

**6.1.1
Question and answer as a practice technique**

Question and answer practice is one of the commonest – and perhaps most overworked – ways of giving language practice in the classroom. It is also one of the most misused. The following basic points in connection with it need to be noted.

(a) *It is only one of many ways of giving practice (whether oral or written).* Some alternatives have been discussed in the previous chapter; other possibilities when exploiting a text are listed in 6.2. Visual aids also enable us to elicit responses from the students in whatever form we want. This makes it possible to get closer to a more natural use of language in the classroom. After all, we do not spend all our time in real life asking and answering questions.

(b) *Questions must be as realistic as possible.* Normally they are requests for information (although we sometimes ask people to confirm what we already known or can see): the person who asks a question expects to be told something that he did not know. Many questions asked in the classroom (e.g. about visual material such as the picture in 5.4) would be treated with scorn in real life, although students tolerate them because they understand that such questions are based on a convention. We should, however, try to exploit simple 'information gap' techniques such as the ones in 5.4.1 and 5.4.2 as much as possible.

(c) *Questions based on a text must not be worded in language that is more difficult than the text itself, or call for answers that are more difficult.* For example, with reference to the dialogue in 4.3.3, you could not, at this level, ask: *When is the carnival going to be held?* in order to elicit: *On May 1st.* The example may seem absurd, but such questions are often asked. To avoid situations like this, therefore, questions (as well as possible answers) have to be worked out beforehand.

(d) *Different ways of asking and answering questions must be taken into account.* The principal ways of asking and answering questions are as follows:

(i) *wh*-questions e.g. *Where is the carnival? When is the carnival?*

(ii) questions formed with an auxiliary verb e.g. *Is Tina a good singer?*

(iii) tag questions e.g. *The carnival is on May 1st, isn't it? Tim can play the guitar, can't he?*

(iv) alternative type questions e.g. *Is the first prize at the carnival £100 or £200?*

The actual choice of questions is likely to be influenced by a number of considerations. For example, how much do you want to help the students towards the answer at any given point of practice? Type (i) appears to do this less than the others, so you will probably want to ask a number of easy questions first to familiarise the students with the text. In any case, you will probably want to vary the question forms e.g. *The carnival is in Greenhill, isn't it? And when is it? And is the first prize £100 or £200?*

Another consideration is whether any of the question types seems to offer better opportunities for meaningful practice. For example, Type (i) requires the students to provide some information from the text which is not in the question (in other words, they cannot simply guess the answer). Type (iii), too, which invites agreement or disagreement, would appear to be more true to life than Type (ii).

We must also take into account what kind of answer we want to elicit from the students. The first type of question may be answered with either a sentence or a phrase. For example: *When is the carnival? It's on May 1st* or: *May 1st.* Since both answers are acceptable, it is wrong to ask for a 'complete' answer. If you want the students to practise responses in the form of sentences, you must find other ways of eliciting them, e.g. *The carnival is on May 2nd.* The students can then contradict you by saying: *No, it isn't. It's on May 1st.*

Question types (ii) and (iii) can be answered in a variety of ways ranging from *Yes (it is)* to *That's right. It's on May 1st* (in answer to the question: *When is the carnival?*). In the early stages we will probably want to give the students plenty of practice in answering with short form answers (*Yes, it is/No, she can't* etc.) since this is an important idiomatic feature of English, but it would be wrong to insist on questions always being answered in one way. More important is to *expose* the students to a variety of answers when *you* answer questions. This is something we noted could be done when playing guessing games (see 5.4.1).

Finally, the obvious point needs to be made that you should not ask all the questions yourself. The students need practice too! If the students are still learning a particular question form, practice might go along these lines:

(a) Ask a question. Get the students to answer it.

(b) Elicit a question (i.e. use a keyword or some other kind of prompt). Get the students to ask a question and answer it yourself.

(c) Get the students to ask one another questions and to answer them.

6.2 Exploiting texts for oral practice

In this section examples are given of ways of exploiting a prose text for oral practice. Dialogue texts can usually be exploited in the same way, although they sometimes also offer, by getting the students to identify with the speakers, opportunities for controlled roleplay.

The sample text below is one based on the same theme as in 4.4.

What happened to the dinosaurs?

A hundred million years ago there were a lot of dinosaurs in the world. Some lived on land. Some lived in the sea. Some could fly. A lot of them were very big, and some had horns or long teeth like the monsters in films. Most of the dinosaurs were plant-eaters, but some of them could kill and eat very big animals.

The world was full of dinosaurs for 135 million years. 60 million years ago, however, they were all dead. What happened to them?

The dinosaurs could not live in a cold climate. 100 million years ago the world was not a very cold place, but some scientists say that about 65 million years ago the world's climate changed. The new climate was cold and this cold climate killed the dinosaurs.

Now we can see dinosaur bones in museums, but we cannot see a real dinosaur.

(a) *Question and answer practice*

Examples of questions and answers, particularly to show how you can vary the types of questions, are given below in the form of a sequence.

Teacher	*Students*
Now, . . . did the dinosaurs live a long time ago?	Yes, they did. A very long time ago.
How long ago? Do you remember?	Yes. A hundred million years.
Yes. A hundred million years ago.	
That was a very long time, wasn't it?	
And were there a lot of them?	Yes.

And they all lived on land, didn't they?	No, not all of them.
Where did they live, then?	Some lived on land. Some lived in the sea. And some . . .
Ah, yes, they could fly. They lived in the air. Not all the time, of course!	
Now, were all the dinosaurs big?	No, but a lot of them were very big.
Yes, they were like monsters, weren't they?	Yes. A lot of them had horns and big teeth.
What did they eat, then? Did they eat other animals?	No, most of them ate plants.
But some could eat other animals, couldn't they?	Yes. They could kill and eat big animals.

The procedure outlined above is useful if you want to 'talk' your way through a text with the class.

(b) *Other techniques for oral practice*

In addition to or as an alternative to question and answer practice, there are various other ways in which a text can be exploited for oral practice. These are set out and illustrated below. It is not suggested that you should use all these devices to exploit a single passage, but rather that you should select one or two which seem to be particularly productive when applied to a given text.

Because some of the activities are open-ended, it will sometimes happen that the first student who responds may not give all the necessary information. In this case other students can be called upon to add to the first answer until an acceptable one has been built up. Some examples of this procedure are given in (i) and (iii) below.

(i) *Right/wrong statements*

The students are asked to say whether a statement is right or wrong within the context of the text. If it is wrong, they are asked to give the correct version.

T: Is this right or wrong? Listen. *Most dinosaurs did not eat animals.* What do you think, . . .?
A: It's right.
T: Do you agree, . . .?
B: Yes. It's right.
T: Yes. It says: *Most of the dinosaurs were plant-eaters.* They ate plants. They did not eat meat. Now, what about this sentence? *All dinosaurs lived on land.* Is it right or wrong, . . .?
C: It's wrong. Some of them lived on land.
T: What do you think, . . .?
D: It's wrong. They didn't all live on land.
T: Good.

(ii) *Corrections*

The students are asked to correct statements.

Examples: *Dinosaurs lived a million years ago* (Response: They lived 135 million years ago). *All dinosaurs were big* (Response: A lot of them were big).

51

(iii) *Expanding statements*

The students have to give more information about a particular item in the text.

T: Now, I want you to give me more details about these things. Listen. *A long time ago there were dinosaurs in the world.* Can you tell me more about dinosaurs?
A: Yes. They lived a hundred million years ago.
T: Good. So what can we say now, ...?
B: A hundred million years ago there were dinosaurs in the world.
T: And were there many dinosaurs?
C: Yes. There were a lot of them!
T: All right, ... Give me a new sentence.
D: A hundred million years ago there were a lot of dinosaurs in the world.

(iv) *Giving reasons*

The students have to explain the point of a statement.

Examples: *Some dinosaurs were like monsters!* (Response: They had horns and long teeth.) *There are no dinosaurs in the world today.* (Response: They are all dead!)

(v) *Stating consequences*

The students have to say what happened as a result of the event or action they hear described. Example: *The world's climate changed.* (Response: The dinosaurs died.)

Other kinds of text-based activity for oral practice will depend on the type of text being exploited. For example, with narrative texts, you can get the students to say what event happened after another, thus leading them to re-tell part of the story. With dialogues, you can get them to identify the speaker (i.e. *Who said this?*) and, depending on the level of the students, to say why he said it.

Discussion

1 What advantages and disadvantages are there in using a text as a context for oral work at the practice stage?
2 Do you agree that question and answer practice is an overworked and often misused technique for oral work? What are the advantages and disadvantages of other techniques (true/false, completion etc.)?

Exercises

1 Choose any text (dialogue or prose passage) and show how it could be exploited for oral practice along the lines of 6.2.
2 Give other ways of exploiting a text for controlled oral practice which you have found useful.
3 Examine any textbook to see if the exercises based on the presentation text are intended to develop either reading skills or oral skills.

References

For guidance on the exploitation of texts see the introductions in the teacher's book for any series of coursebooks such as *Strategies* (Longman); *Streamline* (OUP); *Encounters* (Heinemann); *Track* (Longman) (etc.).

7

From Practice to Production

So far at the practice stage we have been looking at activities which are wholly or mainly under your control. That is to say, you have been working with the whole class together, using drills which give the learners an opportunity to reproduce what they have learned accurately and enabling you to check whether they are able to do this. Only occasionally have they worked on their own, in pairs.

However, an important feature of the production stage is that the learners should work as much as possible on their own, talking to one another directly and not through the medium of the teacher. What is needed, then, as a first step, is a transition phase where the learners get plenty of guidance (either with language or ideas or both) but at the same time are given the chance to talk to one another without constant supervision – or correction – from you.

Two things are needed to put this into effect:

(a) a change from whole class practice to pairwork;
(b) appropriate activities for the students to do.

This transition phase from practice to production is very important. It will provide the learners with the maximum amount of meaningful practice. At the same time, it will get them used to working on their own, which not all learners accept or do well at the start.

7.1.1
Two types of
pairwork

In addition to what we might call 'open pairwork', where the students work informally across the class with one another, asking and answering questions, for example, under your supervision, we can identify two other ways of getting the learners to work in pairs:

(a) *fixed pairs* Each student completes an activity with the same partner. Subsequently they may change partners, either to repeat the activity or to extend it (e.g. by reporting something). Normally the students work with a neighbour for this type of pairwork.

(b) *flexible pairs*   For this each student interacts with a number of students in turn in order to complete a task. This type of pairwork normally requires the students to move freely around the classroom, and can therefore cause problems in large classes. The procedure can be modified, however, so that the students interact only with those in their vicinity, without moving around.

**7.1.2
Procedures for
pairwork**

If pairwork is to be successful (i.e. go off smoothly and result in learning), certain procedures need to be followed.

(a) *Make sure the students know exactly what they have to do.* That is, explain the activity and practise as necessary with 'open' pairs across the class.

(b) *Divide the students into pairs* (taking advantage as much as possible of the way they are seated). A 'pair' may consist of three students. In this case, the third student listens while the other two practise. The students then change partners. In any case, depending on the type of activity, make sure that students take it in turns to initiate and respond (e.g. ask and answer questions).

(c) *Carry out selective checking* i.e. by walking round the class and listening in. Join in with a pair from time to time, especially with those students who are likely to need your help. If you feel that an activity is going badly, stop it, re-present it to the class and let the students start again.

(d) *Control noise level* by stopping an activity and asking the students to start again more quietly.

(e) *Gauge the amount of time* an activity should go on for. Stop the activity when most students have had a reasonable amount of practice. You cannot expect all students to go at exactly the same pace and some students will naturally get more practice than others.

(f) *Provide any necessary feedback.* That is, tell the students how well they have done. If necessary, re-teach any items now or later.

**7.2
Examples of
pairwork
activities**

This is just a selection of the many kinds of pairwork activities you could use at this transition phase. Note that many could be equally well done in groups. However, it is assumed that pairwork is on the whole more suitable, partly because you want the students to do as much talking as possible and partly because it is usually easier to divide a class up into pairs.

**7.2.1
Mini-dialogues**

These are short conversations between two (or possibly three speakers), which provide the learners with models of spoken language. For example:

A: What are you doing tonight?
B: Nothing, really. Why?
A: Why don't we have a game of tennis, then?
B: OK. I'll see you about five.

Such dialogues usually incorporate one or more structures or functions which the learners need to practise, together with any relevant vocabulary. They can also usefully include many features of spoken language (e.g. short-form answers, question tags, hesitation markers such as *Well*, ... and *Er*, ...). In short, they are ideal for those occasions when you want to give the learners controlled practice (although, as we shall see, there are ways of relaxing our control over what they say), especially with a view to getting them used to working together and at the same time increasing their confidence in being able to say *something* in English.

However, it would be wrong to overestimate their effectiveness. If the dialogues are closely modelled, they can be done without very much attention and the learners need not really listen to one another while they are practising. In fact, they are simply *speaking* rather than *talking*.

Here are some ways of providing practice through mini-dialogues.

(a) *Picture sets*

A set of 4–8 pictures, like the one on the right, is a kind of visual substitution table.

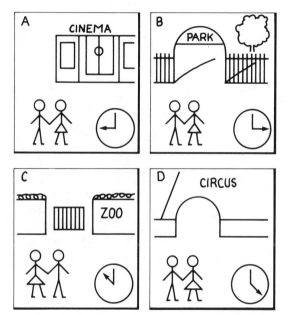

The general structure of each picture is the same (two people going to a place at a certain time) but the actual details are varied: e.g. the places and the times. This enables the students to reproduce new versions of each dialogue with the help of the other pictures in the set. For example, at a very basic level:

Picture A   A: Where are John and Ann?
               B: They said they were going to the cinema.
               A: Really? When did they go?
               B: Oh, at about nine, I think.

Picture B   A: Where are Steve and Joan?
               B: They said they were going to the park.
               A: Really? When did they go?
               B: Oh, at about three, I think.

Some points to note:

(i) The students can talk *about* the picture, as in the example above, or *through* it i.e. do a simple roleplay. E.g.

A: I'm going to the cinema tonight.
B: Are you? Who with?
A: Ann!
B: Gosh! Lucky you!

(ii) The students can work with single exchanges or longer dialogues as required. E.g.

A: Let's go to the cinema.
B: All right. I'll meet you there at about nine.

A: I'm going to the cinema tonight.
B: Oh, can I come too?
A: Certainly not!
B: Why not?
A: Well, I'm going with Tina, that's why.
B: Lucky you!

(iii) The dialogues can relate to two pictures. E.g.

A: Let's go to the cinema, shall we?
B: But we went *there* last night!
A: All right. What would *you* like to do, then?
B: Well, I'd rather go to the park.

The next dialogue will bring in *zoo* and *circus* (although you can of course let the students link any two pictures).

(iv) The pictures can be used just as a stimulus for dialogue practice (i.e. the dialogue relates only loosely to the context). E.g.

A: Seen Bill?
B: Yes. He's gone to the cinema with Ann.
A: Not again!
B: Well, that's *his* business, isn't it?

It should be clear from the examples that a few picture sets can be used to provide a great deal of relevant practice at different levels.

Suggested procedure for using picture sets:

(i) Practise the model dialogue with the whole class, first of all in chorus and then in pairs across the class.

(ii) If necessary, write the model dialogue on the board. If you do this at the repetition stage, you can delete successive portions of the dialogue as the students repeat it. Note, however, that you may need to leave a copy on the board while the students are practising on their own.

(iii) Practise parallel dialogues as necessary. The students may sometimes need or want to write these out. Do whatever you think is best for your class.

(iv) Divide the class into pairs and follow the procedures for pairwork.

(b) Model dialogue and keywords

The students may be asked to work with a single dialogue together with a list of keywords which they can use to produce different versions of the dialogue. However, a more interesting approach is to give them a set of 4–5 dialogues, all of which relate to the same theme. The set below provides practice in talking about occupations.

bank clerk	TV announcer
truck driver	tourist guide
car mechanic	library assistant
air hostess	income tax inspector
traffic warden	fashion model
pop singer	hotel receptionist
football referee	secretary
insurance agent	.... ?

A: Er, what does your (sister) do, then?
B: Works as *(a library assistant)*.
A: (She) likes it, I imagine.
B: Yes, (she's) had the same job ever since (she) left school.

A: You're *(a secretary)* aren't you?
B: Not any more.
A: What do you do now, then?
B: I've got myself a job as *(a hotel receptionist)*.

A: Does your (brother) still work as *(a truck driver)*?
B: No, (he) gave that up. (He's) *(a car mechanic)* now.
A: Is (he)! And how's (he) getting on?
B: Oh, fine.

A: You remember I said I wanted to be *(an air hostess)*?
B: Yes. What about it?
A: I think I'd rather be *(a fashion model)* instead.
B: Are you *sure* that's what you *really* want to be?

A: Well, now you've got your degree, what are you going to be?
B: *(An insurance agent)*.
A: *(An insurance agent)*! But you don't need a degree to be *(an insurance agent)*.
B: I know that. But I'm going to start at the bottom and work my way up!

(c) *Single object picture cards*

This is a very simple but effective way of providing a visual stimulus for dialogue work. A minimum of 6–8 cards will be needed. You can use either large cards (i.e. flashcards), which can be displayed on the board at the front of the class, or give the students small individual cards like those below.

With a set of cards like the ones above, you can get the students to practise a whole range of dialogues like these:

A: Can I have (the clock), please.
B: Yes. Here you are.
A: Can I have (the book), too?
B: No, sorry. You can't have that.

Or:

A: I've just been shopping.
B: Did you buy anything interesting?
A: Well, I bought (a new book).

See 7.2.2 for other uses of picture cards at this stage.

(d) *Gapped dialogues*

These are dialogues where one of the speakers has to supply the missing utterances. E.g.

A: Like to come out tonight?
B: ...
A: How about tomorrow, then?
B: ...
A: OK. See you about (eight), then.
B: ...

Although B is obliged to refuse A's invitation to come out that night because of the way the dialogue has been structured, the student can choose the actual way he responds: e.g. *Not really/Sorry, I'm busy/I can't. I've got a lot to do* (etc.). The speaker's missing words may also be cued by indicating what functions he has to express. E.g.

A: ... *(Invite somebody to go out with you.)*
B: Sorry, I'm busy.
A: ... *(Suggest another day.)*
B: Yes, that would be fine.
A: ... *(Suggest a time.)*
B: All right. See you then.

(e) *Mapped dialogues*

For these the students are given a chart which tells them which functions they must use when they are interacting. For example:

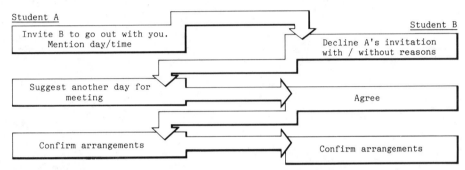

Although this way of providing a framework for language practice may seem attractive, not all students find it easy to interpret these maps and charts and to interact easily. You may find it necessary to give plenty of whole class practice before asking the students to work in pairs.

(f) *Cuewords*

For this the students are given cards with a number of cuewords on them, around which a dialogue can be modelled. For example:

> *job*
> *factory*
> *make shoes*
> *boring/well paid*

The students would also need to be given a model dialogue to work with at the start (at least for the kind of work we have in mind at this stage), with the help of which they could use their cards to talk like this:

A: Hi! I haven't seen you lately.
B: No. I've got a job – at last!
A: Where?
B: In a factory. I make shoes.
A: Really? What's it like?
B: Oh, it's boring, but it's well paid!

7.2.2
Picture cards

These can be given to the students either as sets of individual cards (like those in 7.2.1 c) or in the form of a picture sheet, like the one below.

The picture sheet is obviously easier for the students to handle. For some activities, however, it is useful to have sets of individual cards so that, for example, the students can share out the cards.

One of the most productive uses for picture cards at this stage is to cue mini-dialogues, as discussed in 7.2.1. Some other possible uses are:

(a) *Finding uses*

For example, for the scissors:

$$\text{You can cut} \begin{cases} hair \\ paper \\ cloth \\ \ldots\ldots \end{cases} \text{with them.}$$

You can ask the students to find uses for an object within a particular environment (e.g. park, school, etc.) or to compare the uses for an object in two environments (e.g. a shop and a restaurant). You can also ask the students to find two uses for each object: one normal, practical use, the other absurd. Even controlled language activities of this kind can be very imaginative.

(b) *Association activities*

The students have to link any two objects e.g. in terms of use, colour, material etc. E.g.

scissors/knife   You can cut things with them.
                    They are both made of metal.

Other ways of linking objects are:

You can *break* the radio with the hammer.
You can *hide* the ball in the saucepan. (etc.)

(c) *Classifying objects*

Simple ways of doing this are to group things according to: what they are made of; whether they are used in the house; whether they are modern inventions; whether you can put them in your pocket; whether children use them; whether there is one in the room (etc.).

(d) *Grading objects*

The students can be asked to grade the objects according to whether they think they are:

heavy	light
cheap	expensive
long	short
big	small
useful	not useful

Other uses for picture cards are given under *Language games* in the next section. See (a) and (b) below.

7.2.3
Language games

The games in this section are all either controlled or presented in a controlled version. This makes them suitable for pairwork, although many of them could equally well be done with teams or in groups.

(a) *Find the right picture*

One student 'thinks' of one of the pictures (i.e. he does not tell his partner which one he has chosen). The other tries to find out which one it is by asking *yes/no* type questions. For example, if A has chosen *pen*, his partner can ask: *Is it big?* (No)/*Can you cut things with it?* (No)/*Is there one in this room?* (Yes) (etc.) until he feels he knows the object and can ask: *Is it the pen?*

(b) *'Desert Island'*

This is a basic version of a game which can be exploited in much greater depth for groupwork (see 9.3.2 (b)). The setting for the game is the same, however: the students are told that they are going to have to spend (three) months on a desert island, where there is fresh water and vegetation. They are asked to choose (three) things to take with them and to say what they are going to do with each thing. E.g. (using the picture sheet on page 60):

A: I'm going to take a knife, a radio and a ball.
B: What are you going to do with the knife?
A: Lots of things! I'm going to cut my food with it. I'm going to cut wood with it, too.
B: What about the radio?
A: I'm going to listen to music.
B: Are you going to listen to the news?
A: No. I don't want to hear the news!
B: What are you going to do with the ball?
A: I'm going to play football.
B: But you are alone!
A: It doesn't matter. I want to practise!
Now, what are *you* going to take? (etc.)

The game can be restructured to use the past tense, e.g. *I took* ... / *What did you do with them*?

(c) *Hide and seek*

For this the students 'hide' an object (or themselves) somewhere in a picture like the one below. They then take it in turns to find out where the object has been hidden by asking questions like: *Is it on the bookcase? Is it under the TV?* (etc.) Guessing can be limited by numbering certain positions in the picture.

(d) *Building up descriptions*

The students take turns to build up a description of an object by each adding a sentence. For example, a description of a monster.

A: This monster has got a long neck.

B: It's got a long neck and it has also got big teeth.

A: It's got a long neck and big teeth. And it's got a long tail!

B: It's got a long neck and big teeth. It's got a long tail and it's got wings, too! (etc.)

(e) *Word games*

The students can work together in pairs to see how many words they can make out of one long word. For example:

IMPORTANT

Some possible words: an, or, to, map, ran, ant, not, top, man (etc.).

The language used for doing this can be very simple. E.g. *We can make . . . How about . . .? How do you spell . . .?*

There are a number of simple board games which the students can draw on a sheet of paper from a model on the board.

(f) *Shopping*

The board is made up of 18 squares, arranged in the form of a hollow rectangle. There is the name of a shop on every third square. The students can put these in any order they like.

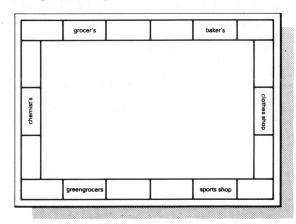

To start, the players place their counters on any blank square. They throw a dice to move and go round the board in a clockwise direction.

For a simple version of the game, the players have only to 'visit' each of the six shops (i.e. by landing on them as they move round and round the board). The first player to visit all six shops is the winner.

For a more difficult version of the game, the players can be asked to name an object which they can buy at the shop they land on. The players get a point for each correct item. The game stops after an agreed number of moves or a set time.

(g) *Places*

The board for this is very similar to the one in (f), except that there are no blank squares.

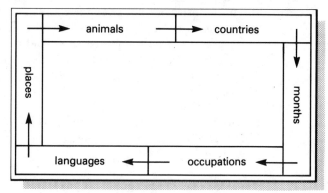

The players can start on any square. They then throw a dice and move round the board in a clockwise direction. When they land on a square (e.g. languages) they can be asked by their partner to spell the name of a language or to give the names of an agreed number of languages (e.g. three). A point is awarded for each correct answer. The winner is the player with most points after (say) five minutes or twenty moves.

(h) *Clothes*

There are 20 squares on this board. The four corner squares are left blank. On the remaining squares the players write the name of a colour and an item of clothing alternately, as shown in the top line.

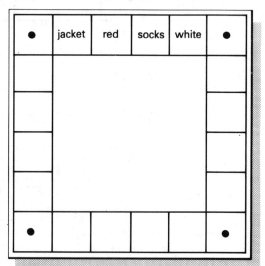

The object of the game is to win six different items of clothing and six colours (which need not be different).

To play the game, the players place a counter on any blank corner square and throw a dice to move round the board in a clockwise direction. They should write down the names of their clothes and colours as shown in the diagram below. They can accumulate colours and clothes and match them later if they prefer.

COLOURS	CLOTHES
red brown blue	socks

The first player to complete his list of six clothes and colours is the winner.

7.2.4
Decision-making
activities

What the following activities have in common is that they require the students to make certain decisions. They also employ the 'information gap' principle: that is, the students have to try to find out something (in this case, what each has decided).

(a) *Picture completion*

For this activity, the students could be given a complete environment, like the room scene on page 62, and asked to decide where to place (ten) objects. Alternatively, they can work with incomplete environments, like the park scene below. In this case, they have to complete the picture themselves, and since there are fewer points of reference, finding out where the objects are is more challenging.

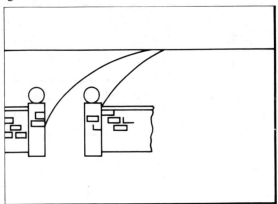

Note the two ways of setting up this activity:

(i) The students copy the scene from one drawn on the board or are given copies of it. They are then told which objects to locate in their picture. E.g. for the park scene, they could be given a list like this:

> 3 trees (1 small)
> pond, small hut,
> 2 seats, dog
> 4 people (2 children)

65

They can also be allowed to omit any (three) objects from their list. When they draw their pictures (which of course they do without showing them to one another), clearly there will be a lot of differences.

For this activity the students will normally interact by asking questions in order to find out what each one's picture looks like. E.g.

A: Where have you put your trees?
B: One is near the gate.
A: Is it big or small?
B: Big. And it's on the left of the gate.
A: All right. So you've one big tree on the left of the gate.
   Now, where are the other trees?
B: They are in the top left-hand corner of the park.
A: OK. Now, what about the pond?
B: That's near the trees – on the left.
A: Good. And is the hut there, too?
B: No. I haven't drawn a hut (etc.).

Street plans can also be used for this type of activity. The students have only to write the numbers of the places on the map to indicate their positions. They can of course be left to choose the positions for themselves.

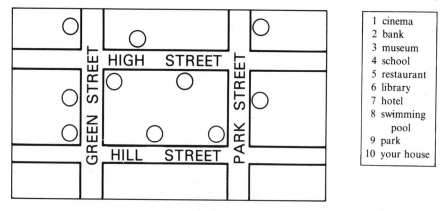

| 1 cinema |
| 2 bank |
| 3 museum |
| 4 school |
| 5 restaurant |
| 6 library |
| 7 hotel |
| 8 swimming pool |
| 9 park |
| 10 your house |

(ii) Alternatively, the students may be given folders with the environments mounted inside them, as shown in the diagram below, together with a set of small object cards. Each pair of students normally has identical sets (although you can choose to introduce some differences, as for the 'park' activity above, where the students were allowed to omit some items).

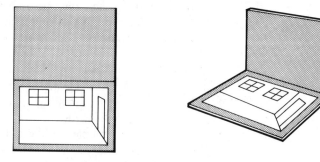

While the students are arranging their scenes, and also while they are interacting, the blank half of the folder serves as screen between the players (as shown in the right-hand picture).

For this version of the activity, the players can interact in a variety of ways:

– They can build up their pictures step by step. E.g.

A: I'm going to put my bookcase under the window.

B: I'm going to put mine near the door.

Or:

A: I'm going to put my lamp on the bookcase.
Put yours on the bookcase too.

– A positions all his objects. He then tells B how to arrange his in the same way. This usually involves quite a bit of questioning on the part of B in order to establish the exact positions.

– A positions all his objects. B then tries to find out where each object is and arranges his environment in the same way.

– Both players arrange their scenes simultaneously. They then compare their scenes by talking about them. E.g.

A: I've put my table in the middle of the room.
Where have you put yours?

(b) *Non-pictorial aids*

Non-pictorial aids such as maps, menus, radio and TV programmes are another effective way of getting the students to interact using fairly controlled language.

For example, with maps the students can practise giving directions how to get from one place to another. They will need a good deal of whole class preparation with appropriate language first (language difficulties in this area are often underestimated). Controlled pairwork practice of the kind envisaged at this stage will then be very useful preparation for more open roleplay-type situations at a later stage.

With menus, the students can (at this stage) simply decide what they are going to have to eat and drink (perhaps taking into account a certain sum of money which they have been given to spend). If three students are working together, they can also practise simple conversations that involve ordering from the menu.

RENDEZVOUS

HOT DISHES		DRINKS	
Fish & chips	£1.10	Milk	20p
Sausages & chips	90p	Tea	22p
Egg & chips	80p	Coffee	25p
Chips	35p	Milkshake	25p
		Seven Up	20p
		Lemonade	22p
SANDWICHES		Coca Cola	22p
Cheese	35p		
Tomato	35p		
Egg	40p	ICECREAMS	
Cheese & tomato	45p	Chocolate	35p
Bread & butter	15p	Strawberry	35p
		Vanilla	35p
CAKES			
Buns	15p		
Plain cake	18p		
Chocolate cake	25p		
Fruit cake	22p		

With TV and radio programmes like those below the students can discuss what they are going to watch/listen to or what they actually did watch/listen to the previous evening. E.g.

TV Channel 2

6.00	Science Our World
6.50	Sports Report
7.15	Cartoon Tom and Jerry
7.25	NEWS
7.45	Film Adventure in Space
9.00	NEWS
9.30	Kojak

Radio One

6.00	History The Aztecs (Part 4)
6.30	Tonight's Short Story: The Dreamer
6.40	Top Twenty
7.45	The Book Programme
8.10	Animal World
8.45	NEWS

A: What are you going to do tonight?

B: I'm going to watch *Sports Report* at six-fifty. Then I'm probably going to listen to *Animal World* at ten past eight. How about you?

Or:

A: I watched *Adventure in Space* last night.

B: What was it like?

A: Fantastic!

The students can also work out a whole evening's viewing and listening and then compare their decisions. Alternatively, they can be asked to work out together a joint programme which is acceptable to both.

(c) *Agendas*

For this the students need to make or be given a page from a diary like the one below.

Student A

	MORNING	AFTERNOON
MON		Dentist
TUES	Help at home	
WED		
THURS	Shopping	Dentist
FRI		visit aunt
SAT	Shopping	

Student B

	MORNING	AFTERNOON
MON	Doctor's	
TUES		Shopping
WED		Dentist
THURS	Help at home	
FRI	Shopping	Theatre
SAT		

Each student is asked to fill in half the available slots with obligations of some kind (e.g. shopping, dentist, visit aunt). They then interact to try to find some free time when they can meet to do something pleasurable, such as play tennis, go for a walk (etc.).

A: Let's play tennis together next week.
B: That's a nice idea. Are you free on Monday afternoon?
A: Sorry. I've got to go to the dentist.
   What about Tuesday afternoon.
B: No, I'm not free then. I'm going shopping.
   Are you free on Wednesday morning?
A: Yes, I am.
B: Good! Let's meet, then. And what about Thursday afternoon? (etc.)

7.2.5 Questionnaires and quizzes

(a) Questionnaires

Questionnaires, like the ones below, are a simple way of giving the students meaningful question and answer practice. Although a feature of many textbooks, you can in fact ask the students to write their own.

	TOM	ANN
bread	YES	
cake	YES	
jam	NO	
fish	YES	

	ANN	TOM
run	never	
swim	often	
play tennis	sometimes	
dance	very often	

Questionnaires for use at this stage should usually relate to a topic of some kind, e.g. likes and dislikes about food, activities, abilities (etc.). The answer required should be either *yes* or *no*, or one of the frequency adverbs (*never, hardly ever, sometimes, quite often, regularly* etc.), as for the second questionnaire above.

If the students are going to write their own questionnaires, it is helpful to elicit some ideas from the class first and perhaps write these on the board. Then ask the students to make up their own questionnaires, using some of these items. They can work in pairs for this, thus providing an additional source of talk. They may interview more than one student. They can also be asked to report what they have learned either to another student or to the whole class.

(b) *Quizzes*

Quizzes are similar to questionnaires but the answers to them are usually factual, i.e. they involve knowledge. The examples below relate to other students in the class and general knowledge (which might have been taken from reading texts in the coursebook).

1 What is Lucy's telephone number ?
2 Has George got any brothers ?
3 Where does Tom live ?

1 What's the capital of Turkey ?
2 What language do they speak in Egypt?
3 Where is Mount Olympus ?
4 What's the longest river in the world?
5 What's the capital of India ?
6 Can horses see colours ?

To turn quiz writing into an oral practice activity, you must ask the students to work in pairs to produce the quiz. This will involve talking. Each pair should then ask another pair of students to answer the quiz orally.

**7.2.6
Flexible pairwork**

As we noted in 7.1.1, ideally, for activities like the ones below, the students should be allowed to move around the classroom and to interact freely with other students in the classroom. In practice, however, most of these activities work quite well if the students remain seated and interact only with those who are near them.

(a) *Questionnaires*

The type of questionnaire used for this activity is different from the ones in 7.2.5. Basically it involves identifying somebody who corresponds to a requirement of the questionnaire. For example, the questionnaire may read:

Find someone who:	N A M E
– is wearing black socks	
– likes flying	
– can't swim	
– has never been abroad	
– would like to go to the moon	

When the student with the questionnaire finds someone who answers *yes* (or *no* if the requirement is a negative one), he writes that person's name in the right-hand column.

Questionnaires can focus on a single structure. E.g.

Find someone who:	NAME
– can speak three languages	
– can use a computer	
– can make cakes	
– can ride a horse	
– can't ride a bike	

Questionnaires of the first type (i.e. with mixed structures) are effective ways of getting students to draw on all their language resources, although you may need to indicate to the students the range of tenses (etc.) that they could use. For maximum talk, get the students to collaborate on the construction of the questionnaires.

(b) *Find your partner*

For this activity each student in the class needs a card with a picture on it. Each set of cards is made up of pairs of identical pictures. All other cards in the set are similar but contain at least one difference. Thus matching cards in the complete set (of which some examples only are given below) will show:

– houses with the same number of doors (one or two)

– the same colour door or doors

– houses with the same number of windows (one, two or three)

– the same number of trees in the garden (one or two).

In order to find a partner, each student has to move around the class, asking questions. Student A, in the dialogue below, is trying to find someone who has a card identical to his.

A: Excuse me, how many doors has your house got?
B: Two.
A: Oh, my house has only got one. Thanks a lot. Goodbye!

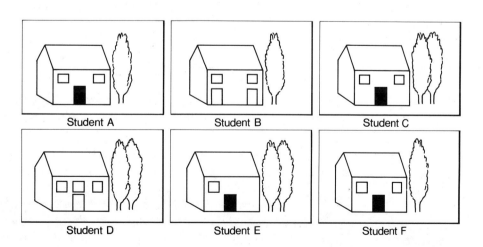

| Student A | Student B | Student C |
| Student D | Student E | Student F |

A then stops someone else.

A: Excuse me, how many doors has your house got.
C: One.
A: Good. My house has got one too. What colour is it?
C: Green.
A: Really! My house has got a green door too.
C: How many windows are there?
A: Two.
C: My house has got two windows, too!
   How many trees are there in the garden?
A: One.
C: One. Oh, there are two in my garden. What a pity!
A: Well, goodbye. Thanks a lot.

A (and B and C too, of course) then continues his search for a partner. He talks to D and E – and finally finds that F has an identical card. As you can see, although it is possible for students to find a partner quite quickly, they normally have to ask a lot of questions before they meet the person with the matching card.

(c) *Let's go together*

This is in fact a decision-making activity which then involves, like the activity above, finding a partner, i.e. someone who has made the same decision. The information the students need for this activity can be presented in tabular form on the board. Two examples are given below.

July	August	September
London	Brighton	Edinburgh
Park Hotel	Palace Hotel	Castle Hotel

For the first activity, each student is asked to decide (without telling anyone else):

– which month he is going on holiday
– which town he is going to
– which hotel he is going to stay in.

For example, Student A may choose August/London/Castle Hotel; Student B: July/Brighton/Park Hotel (and so on: there are in fact twenty-seven different possibilities!).

The students should write these down so that they do not change their minds or forget what they have decided in the excitement of the activity. They then move around the class asking questions like: *When are you going on holiday?* Or: *Are you going on holiday in August?* Or: *I'm going on holiday in August. How about you?* (etc.) When they meet someone who has made exactly the same decision, they say: *'Fantastic! Let's go together, then!'*

Varig	Alitalia	JAL
London	Cairo	New York
Sunday	Thursday	Friday

This activity is done in the same way. That is, each student chooses the airline he is going to fly on, the place he is going to and the day on which he is going to fly. For example: *Alitalia to London on Friday*. The students then try to find someone who has made a similar choice.

Although these activities are similar to *Find your partner* in (b), there is one big difference. Since the students have to make their own decisions, it is possible that several students will make the same one (so that they should always be encouraged to go on searching even after they have found one partner). It is equally possible, however, that some students will not be able to find anyone to whom they can say: '*Let's go together!*'

Discussion

1 What are the advantages and disadvantages of using pairwork in a large class of learners (i.e. thirty or more)?
2 What steps would you take to ensure that the learners do not make too many mistakes while doing pairwork?
3 Do you think that mini-dialogues provide an effective way of giving oral practice at this 'controlled-to-free' stage?
4 How would you organise flexible pairwork activities so that they do not involve the students in moving round the class? Do you think that such activities are more trouble than they are worth?
5 How important do you think it is to try to provide a transition from controlled to free activities?

Exercises

1 Draw or specify the design for a picture set similar to the example in this chapter. Show how you would use it.
2 Suggest other uses for giving semi-controlled practice with the help of a set of single object picture cards like those on page 60.
3 Make a list of the key activities suggested in this chapter and then examine any textbook to see what use is made of these or similar activities.

References

1 On classroom management, see R Gower and S Walters (1983) Ch 3 and J Harmer (1983) 10.1.
2 For activities at this stage, see:
   – S Holden (ed.) (1978), particularly on the use of visual materials;
   – W Littlewood (1981);
   – P Hubbard et al (1983).
3 For activities (many of which are briefly described in this chapter) see D Byrne *Teacher's Guides to Interaction Package A* (Modern English Publications 1978); *Interaction Package B* (Modern English Publications 1978) and the *Roundabout Teacher's Resource Book* (Modern English Publications 1981).

8

The Production stage

**8.1
The needs of
the learners**

We noted in 1.2.3 that it is part of your job as a teacher to provide the learners with opportunities to *use the language for themselves*: to say what *they* want to say rather than what they are *directed* to say. Here it is important to stress again that we are not thinking of some advanced stage of language learning when – miraculously! – the learners will know enough of the language to be able suddenly to use it fluently in conversation and discussion (for many students this day may never come), but rather of *opportunities that need to be provided regularly at all levels throughout the course*. They are an essential part of the long process of developing fluency.

Admittedly, in the early stages, such opportunities will be more limited and perhaps more contrived: we may only be able to ask the students a few 'personal' questions (*Did you see 'The Thirty-nine Steps' on TV last night? Did you like it?* etc.), or play a few language games with them or invite their halting comments, say, on a picture. What they will be able to say will be very limited and no doubt they will make mistakes. Nevertheless, the opportunity to say *something* has to be given to them, so that they can see for themselves the value and use of what they are learning; to appreciate that language is an *instrument to be used*, not knowledge or information to be stored away.

And the attempt to get them to try to express themselves has to be made because an important aspect of language learning is the need to learn how to make the best use of the little you know; how to accommodate what you know of the language to the situations in which you are required to use it. It is part of your job to show the learners how they can do this *at the present moment* (rather than let them believe that they will be able to do it at some remote date in the future): by giving them examples when talking with the whole class, by providing them with the right opportunities (through groupwork) and, of course, by not discouraging them by overcorrection.

For the learners, this is a vital stage of learning, but they will probably seem to you to lurch backwards and forwards rather than make steady progress. It will not be so easy to measure their performance as it was at the practice stage, when we were concentrating mainly on accuracy. Nor is there any easy recipe for success. What is needed is flexibility, tolerance, patience on your part – and, above all, an understanding of the learners' difficulties.

8.1.1
The problems of
the learners

The problems which the learners have at this stage may be viewed under three headings:

(a) *linguistic* It is sometimes argued that the students do not know enough of the language to express themselves with ease. Free expression therefore will merely tax their limited competence and result in errors which could be avoided if we continued to guide what they said. All this is in a sense true, but largely irrelevant. It has already been pointed out that they must be given opportunities to try out language for themselves and to make the best use of what they know in a variety of situations. It is an essential part of language learning in the classroom. At the same time, however, you will still be helping the learners much of the time, especially through the choice of activities which you ask them to do. Some activities, such as full-scale discussion and simulation, unquestionably belong to the later stages of the language programme, but there are many others (in particular those presented in the next two chapters) which can provide the learners with opportunities to say what they want to say quite early on in the course.

As for mistakes, it is better that they should occur in the classroom, where they provide feedback for remedial teaching (that is, if they do not disappear naturally in the course of further learning) rather than later, when you are no longer in a position to help the students. We need not be unduly worried that students will pick up mistakes through overhearing them in the classroom: learning rarely takes place so easily.

(b) *psychological* There are two main problems to note here. In the first place, although many students are happy to speak in chorus or under your guidance when doing some kind of drill, they are inhibited when they are asked to express themselves freely in the presence of the whole class. This may be because they have never been encouraged sufficiently to 'have a go' – without worrying about mistakes. But in part this may also be due to the fear of being corrected in front of the other students. This situation can be set right in two ways. First, you should avoid unnecessary correction and, when you feel you have to do it, do it obliquely rather than directly, so that the learners perceive their mistakes for themselves. Secondly, provision must be made on an increasing scale for the students to work on their own. A step was made in the right direction through paired practice (7.1). This must now be taken a stage further through group work (see 8.2).

The second problem is that of motivation. How do we select activities which will arouse the interest of the learners and make them want to talk? As we shall see, there is no single answer to this. We shall need a whole range of activities which will involve them on an imaginative, cognitive and, above all, personal level.

(c) *cognitive* Here we must consider the question of providing the learners with something to talk about: a topic, a theme, a problem of some kind. The first thing to note is that the stimulus need not be verbal: a picture (or a set of pictures) may, for example, be far more effective in conveying ideas for the students to talk about. The special role of pictorial aids is discussed below (8.4). Secondly, topics or themes chosen for this purpose should not call for specialised knowledge. If information is needed to arouse talk, it can be provided through a text (heard or read) or through a pictorial aid. What we are especially concerned with is not what the students *know* (although there are occasions when we shall want to draw on their knowledge) but their *opinions and reactions*. As we shall see, pictorial aids can be invaluable in evoking personal responses, especially on an imaginative level.

8.2 Groupwork

At the presentation and practice stages of learning, it is normally both economical and effective to teach the whole class as a single unit – and indeed, even at the production stage, there are many useful things that you can do by interacting with the whole class. However, the class is, after all, a purely arbitrary unit whose size may vary, and to increase the amount of practice the students can get, as well as making it more realistic by getting them to talk to one another, we have already recommended dividing the class up into pairs. Our concern now at the production stage is to provide the students with an environment within which they can communicate easily and freely, and within which they can work together independently with only the minimum amount of direction from you. The solution lies in forming smaller units – or groups. This does not of course mean that you should not or do not need to do pairwork at this stage. In fact, it may sometimes be more convenient (because of time) or more suitable (because of the type of activity). The main advantage, however, in using groups at this stage is that they provide a richer climate for interaction.

How groups are organised is explained in detail in 8.2.1. Here we should note that the group, made up of perhaps 6–8 students under the direction of a group leader (one of the students themselves), whose function it is to coordinate the activities of the group and to serve as required as a link with you, is a largely autonomous unit. You will have to present and perhaps explain (and sometimes demonstrate) the activities which the students are required to do in their groups, but once this has been done, the students should be allowed to work to a large extent on their own. Divided into groups, the students are now able to sit together, facing one another in a small but intimate circle (rather like a club meeting) and talk freely. You will still be present and you will have an important and often demanding role to play in helping and advising the students as required, but you will now be acting as a guide or consultant rather than as a conventional teacher.

Of course we cannot pretend that everything will go smoothly from the start (*difficulties* are also discussed in 8.2.1). Like all procedures – from chorus work, when the students have to work in unison, to pairwork, when they have to begin to work on their own – group activities take some time to get accustomed to. This is true both for the students and for you, the teacher. But the students quickly learn the value of self-directed activity, of being allowed to be 'agents in their own learning'. Above all, they are motivated to go on learning (the importance of which was noted in 1.2.3) because they are made aware that they can use for themselves, on however limited a scale, the language they are learning. It should not be forgotten that for many learners (especially children and adolescents) group activities offer the only opportunity of putting the language to a real and immediate use.

8.2.1
Organising
groupwork

(a) *Forming groups*   The size of the groups should be worked out in relation to the total number of students in the class. As a general rule, we could say that there should be 5–8 students in each group and not more than 5–6 groups in the class. Remember that you will still have to look after the groups (i.e. clear up any difficulties, check that they are working etc.) and it is difficult to 'manage' a large number of groups. You should normally form the groups yourself, usually on the basis of mixed ability (i.e. good and weak students together) since as a rule learners do help one another. However, there will be occasions when you will want the students to work together on tasks which have been selected to suit their abilities. In this case you should form groups from students of more or less equal ability, so that you will be free to give your attention to those who most need your help. Each group should have an identifying label (i.e. name or number) and a set position in the classroom to work in so that, when students are asked to form groups, they can do so with the minimum fuss and delay. Usually groupwork will involve some re-arrangement of the classroom furniture.

(b) *Group leader*   Each group should have its own 'leader' (or coordinator, if that title is preferred). At the start, *you* will probably have to appoint the group leader, but later on the students can be allowed to choose their own. The function of the group leader is not to dominate the group but to coordinate their activities and to serve as a link between the group and you.

(c) *The role of the teacher*   Your role, both in setting up these activities and in overseeing them while they are in progress, is a crucial one and will, of course, be very different from the one you have in more conventional teaching situations. These are some of the things you must do:

(i)   *Select activities carefully*   You should ensure that the activities can be done reasonably well with the language the students have at their disposal. You may have to indicate to the students how they can do this. Sometimes an activity will require new language and you must decide whether you are going to pre-teach this or let the students ask for it when they realise they need it.

(ii)   *Work out the instructions for an activity carefully*   Presenting the activity to the class will be a major factor in its success. Keep instructions simple, and if necessary use the mother tongue.

(iii)   *Present the activity to the class*   As noted above, you may need to do this in the mother tongue, but try to use English as much as possible because both explaining and evaluating activities is a very real use of language in a classroom situation. Give plenty of examples and give the students a 'trial run'.

(iv)   *Monitor the students' performance*   While the activities are in progress, your main task is to move around the class and to 'listen in' discreetly in order to find out how the students are getting on. You may also join in and help with an activity but if you do so, it should be as a member of the group. Do not, as a rule, correct mistakes of language during a group activity but make a note of them and use them as the basis of feedback (see below). The students should also be told that you are available for consultation if they need you, either to clarify instructions or to help with language.

(v) *Provide feedback*   There is no set way of doing this, and in any case it will to some extent depend on the nature of the activity. For example, you may want to evaluate the activity as a whole (e.g. how well the students participated or performed). In this case, it will usually be appropriate to ask them to give their ideas first before giving your opinion. You will also need to establish the students' reactions to an activity (if you are not already aware of this from monitoring). If students react negatively, you may decide not to repeat the activity, to modify it or, if you are convinced of its value, to try to demonstrate why it is important. (Students often misunderstand the value of games, for example. In this case, it may be advisable simply not to use the term 'game'.) A major kind of feedback will be concerned with language. If, during your monitoring of the activities, you have detected mistakes, you may choose to point these out to the group afterwards or, if it seems appropriate, to the whole class. Alternatively, you may use errors you have noted as the basis for remedial or further teaching. While you are monitoring, you will also become aware that the students *could* perform better if they knew certain items of language. Make a note of these and find an opportunity to teach them to the class.

(vi) *Keep a record*   It is important to keep a record of the activities you have done with a class, together with any comments on the students' performance. You should also note down any ideas for further activities which occur to you or modifications of existing ones. These will often occur to you while you are monitoring.

(d) *Duration and frequency*   Many factors are involved here (the number of lessons per week, the level of the class etc.) but, once the students have enough language for communication activities, on however limited a scale, you should try to provide some groupwork about once a week for perhaps half a class period. Longer sessions may sometimes be required (to complete a project, for example, in which the students are especially involved) and in general it is inadvisable to interrupt an activity that is going well.

(e) *Problems*   We will look at these under different headings:

(i) *time*   Some teachers feel dissatisfied because groupwork is time-consuming, and because they cannot see their students making obvious and measurable progress. It is true that progress cannot be measured in the same way as it could at the practice stage, but remember that students are not merely consolidating what they have learned but also using, perhaps for the first time, what they have learned only superficially at earlier stages. This is of great motivational value and offsets the apparent disadvantage that groupwork is time-consuming.

(ii) *lazy students* It is sometimes argued that lazy students will take advantage of groupwork to be even lazier! This may sometimes happen. However, since students usually get more deeply involved in group activities than in regular class work, laziness is not likely to increase.

(iii) *use of the mother tongue* It is inevitable in monolingual groups that students will sometimes resort to the use of the mother tongue: it is, after all, natural if we ask students to *communicate*! There may also be occasions when we might actually ask the students to work in the mother tongue (or at least allow them the option of doing so) in order to achieve something that will lead on to a productive use of English (see especially project work in 11.4). Apart from selecting activities which you can be reasonably sure are not beyond the level of the students and in preparing them if necessary with some essential language (especially in the early stages), there are a number of things you can do to help overcome this problem:
  - explain to the students why they are doing activities of this kind: i.e. that this is an opportunity to *use* English;
  - demonstrate whenever possible how they can 'get round' difficulties i.e. through alternative expressions. (Many students think they cannot say something unless they know the exact word!)
  - encourage the students to consult you if they have real difficulties;
  - ask them – at least from time to time – to impose self-discipline e.g. through a penalty system which requires them to pay a small fine if they use the mother tongue. This can be done in a fun-like way so that the students actually enjoy catching one another out.

You must not expect, however, that the use of the mother tongue will simply disappear. What you must do is balance against this (and other disadvantages) the very real benefit to be gained from working in groups.

(iv) *discipline* There may be problems of discipline from time to time. We have noted how it takes time for students to get used to new procedures. But the real problem in classrooms is not *active* indiscipline or bad behaviour, which can be easily detected and corrected (and in any case tends to disappear when students are involved in learning) but *passive* indiscipline in the form of non-participation, when the students opt out of learning. This, however, is more likely to result from conventional class teaching than from groupwork.

8.2.2
Group activities

Numerous suggestions are made in the following sections. Many language games (see Chapter 9) can also be played in groups, and groupwork will also be needed for roleplay and simulation (see Chapter 10). It should be noted that when the students are organised for work in this way, they can talk to one another and therefore, in discussing an activity (for example, what to put into a dialogue) real conversation is one of the side-products. Generally they will need a fairly concrete project with a well-defined goal (e.g. arriving at an interpretation of a picture, preparing a dialogue for dramatisation). And although they work separately in their groups, the final stage of the activity is not normally reached until the class is re-formed and the students are given the opportunity to show or discuss what they have achieved. The culmination of group activities, therefore, normally takes place within the context of the class as a whole.

Alternatively, if you want to let the students continue working on a group basis, you can get them to form new groups in such a way that each new group contains representatives from all the old groups. For example:

Old:	Group 1			Group 2			Group 3		
	1	2	3	7	8	9	13	14	15
	4	5	6	10	11	12	16	17	18
New:	Group 1			Group 2			Group 3		
	1	2	7	3	4	9	5	6	11
	8	13	14	10	15	16	12	17	18

In this way the students can share their ideas without any intervention on your part. You should gauge carefully, however, which procedure – whole class forum or continued groupwork – is more likely to benefit the students.

8.3 Preparing for and organising discussion

By discussion is meant any exchange of ideas and opinions either on a class basis, with you as the mediator and to some extent as the participator, or within the context of a group, with the students talking amongst themselves. It may last for just a few minutes or it may continue for a whole lesson (in which case it belongs, of course, to an advanced stage of language learning). It may be an end in itself, a technique for getting the students to talk, or it may serve as the preliminary or final stage of some group activity. These conditions will affect the precise requirements for discussion.

However, there are two further factors which will in general determine whether a discussion is a success or a failure:

(a) *the stimulus for discussion* The activity must motivate the students i.e make them want to talk. This may depend to a large extent on how it is presented to them.

(b) *the role of the teacher* What part do you play either in a class discussion or when, occasionally, you participate in one during a group activity? Perhaps in either case your role is not so essentially different. First, we should note, it is not your job to inform or force your opinions on the students but rather to encourage them to express theirs. Your opinion, if offered at all, should only serve to stimulate further ideas on the part of the students, not to inhibit them. Secondly, you should appear to be more interested (and genuinely interested) in their ideas rather than in the way they express them: it is not part of your job at this stage, as we have already noted, to worry about mistakes the students make. Sometimes, of course, you may have to help students to get their message across or make their meaning clear, but this should be done with tact, perhaps by a re-statement of what the speaker has said. Your job as mediator is, after all, to keep the channels of communication open. For that reason you also have the task of keeping the discussion going (at least when it is on a class basis), not of course by doing all the talking yourself, nor by making general observations or addressing questions to no one in particular, but by stimulating one or two students in particular to say something through, for example, a question. Part of your preparation for discussion should therefore be to decide which questions or which points are best addressed to certain students.

Throughout this kind of work your attitude will be of vital importance: you must be informal and relaxed; you must appear interested and you must of course be patient. But, above all, you must be prepared. There is no point in bringing an interesting or attractive visual aid into the classroom in the mere hope that it will spark off discussion spontaneously. You must work out guidelines for its exploitation beforehand – even if discussion ultimately goes off in another direction (as we shall see in 8.4.1, this often happens when students are asked to interpret a picture). Similarly a topic, whether presented visually or through a text of some kind, must be analysed carefully beforehand to identify those features which will help you relate it to the students' interest, background and experience. It is the identification of these, as well as possible related difficulties of language, which will determine to a large extent the ultimate success or failure of a discussion.

8.4
The function of visual aids at the production stage

At the presentation and practice stages visual aids serve mainly to provide a clear contextual setting for the items being taught: either to illustrate their meaning or to elicit responses that relate to what is shown in the picture. This picture, for example, could be used to show the meaning of the statement:

There's a vase of flowers on the table. It could also be used to elicit the same pattern from the students, or for related practice e.g. *Where did I leave the flowers? You left them on the table.* For this purpose we exploit the *visible* features of the picture, and for that reason it is important that those features should at all times be clear. At the production stage, however, although pictures may be used on a referential level (e.g. within the context of a detailed picture such as a scene shown in a wall chart, the students may be asked to describe what they can actually *see*) their main value lies in stimulating interpretation and discussion. It is in this way that we can get the students' *own point of view*. For this purpose we shall want to go beyond what can actually be *seen* in the picture to what is *implied* by it. Although most pictures can be used in this way (for example, even the picture above could be the object of speculation: *Who do you think put the flowers on the table? Why? Did (she) buy them or pick them in the garden? etc.*), it is often necessary to select or design ones whose 'open-endedness' is likely to provide a fertile source of speculation. This approach is discussed and illustrated in 8.4.1. In addition to this, as a group activity, we shall also find good use for pictures which imply dialogue (see 8.4.2.) and for pictures, or sets of pictures, which provide a basis for discussion (see 8.4.3.).

It should be kept in mind that there is nothing *elementary* about visual aids in themselves (although, unfortunately, they tend to be closely associated with the early stages of language learning). It is the *use* we make of them that counts. The importance of visual aids at the production stage is that they offer a *non-verbal* framework for language practice and can therefore be used at different levels of proficiency.

8.4.1.
Pictures for
interpretation

The pictures in this section are not meant to be *described;* if they were approached in this way, their visible features would be rapidly exhausted and all talk would soon be over. Instead, the students should be invited to identify the 'unknown' aspects of the picture: what is implied but not seen. It is these unseen features which will provide a framework for discussion. For example, in the first picture below, we can see a woman looking out of a window. But we do not know *what* she has seen, *where* the object (person or thing) is; *who* she is talking to and *what* she is saying. On each of these points there may be as many as a dozen points of view, and it is precisely this diversity of opinion which will give rise to discussion. Of course, the students are not used to looking at pictures in this way and at the start these points will probably have to be identified for them. But they will soon begin to perceive them for themselves.

The first exploitation of the picture could be carried out as follows:

Step 1   Elicit from the students the guidelines for discussion, such as the ones above. These may be written on the blackboard together with any useful items of language. Avoid putting ideas into the students' heads and discourage them from making up their minds about the picture too quickly.

Step 2 Divide the students into their groups and ask them to discuss the various guidelines. To some extent the actual *talk* that results from this is an end in itself, since the students are using language in a natural way, but they may also be asked to agree on an interpretation acceptable to the whole group. It is impossible to predict how the discussion will go or what bizarre interpretations may be thrown up in the course of it, but the *kind* of language which students at an elementary level might reasonably be expected to use could take the following form:

A: I think she's seen a man ...
B: Where?
A: In the street.
C: What's he doing?
A: Oh, he's just fallen off his bike.
D: But the woman's laughing.
B: She isn't laughing. She's smiling.
D: Well, why is she smiling?
A: Perhaps she doesn't like the man.
E: I don't agree with this. I think ... (etc.).

Step 3 Re-form the class and ask a spokesperson from each group to present the interpretation of his group, which (depending on the amount of time available) is then commented on by the other students in the class, who can ask questions, raise objections etc.

But there are still other uses that can be made of such pictures for oral production. For variety we now turn to the second picture, which we assume has been interpreted in the same way (that is, the students have made their minds up about the following: *who* the woman is; *what time* of day it is; *why* she has a lot of washing-up to do; *why* she has not done it etc.). We may now

set the students roleplay tasks to perform (either as individuals or as part of a group activity). One exercise might be: *You have a lot of washing-up to do: persuade someone to help you!* Or: *You ring up a friend and find that (he) is feeling very depressed* (this is a feature of the picture): *how would you cheer (him) up?*

Notice that in this way we begin to make the picture relate to the students personally. But we must go still further so as to begin to draw on their own experiences. For this purpose an informal class discussion might be initiated by asking the students, for example: *What would you do in this situation? Do you have to help with the washing-up at home? Do you like (mind) it?* From there we might broaden the discussion to talk about 'Women's Lib'. For example: *Are women trying to become more independent in your country? In what way? What is the attitude to this?* etc. Or we might lead the discussion in a different direction (though still related to the picture) to talk about some of the things that the students find depressing: traffic, rising prices, pollution etc.

We should note (referring back to 8.3.) that all these points, as well as the initial exploration of the picture to work out the guidelines, should be *prepared carefully and in some detail before the lesson.* Many of the possibilities afforded by such pictures will be lost unless you are sufficiently well prepared. And it should be remembered that there is not one level of exploitation only. The same picture may be used more than once with a class at different stages of the course. There is in fact great value in doing this because, on each occasion the students use the picture, they should be able to express themselves in more complex language about it. In this sense it provides a kind of gauge of their language growth. Thus the students who could only say at one time (with reference to the first picture in this section): *She is looking out of the window at her children. They are playing in the street* should eventually be able to produce: *Well, she just happened to look out of the window, you see, and she saw a cow eating the flowers in her neighbour's garden!*

Before we leave this way of exploiting pictorial material, you should note that pictures of faces are a particularly fruitful source of discussion – mainly perhaps because in real life too we often wonder about people just from looking at them. Using pictures of faces, then, we can ask the students to decide:

– how old the person is;
– what (his) nationality is;
– whether (he) is married or single;
– what (his) occupation is;
– what (his) interests and hobbies are.

You will find that age and nationality provoke a lot of discussion and provide a natural context for using modal forms (such as: *may/might/could/must be*).

Students tend to like to be given a 'true' biography of the person, so for this activity it is advisable to prepare a version yourself, which you present at the end as the correct one. Students react just as vigorously to being right (*You see! I was right!*) as to being wrong (*That's impossible! I don't believe it!*).

8.4.2
Pictures for
dialogue
production and
role-playing

We have already seen how visual material can be used to produce guided dialogues (see 7.2.1(a)). At this stage, however, we are concerned to stimulate free expression and therefore the amount of guidance the students are given must be accordingly reduced. Also, since the students are now working in groups, they can not only collaborate to produce acceptable dialogues but they must also first discuss the ideas and language to be used. Once again, then, talk is a side product of the activity.

You must therefore gauge carefully the amount of guidance that needs to be given. But where you *must* help the students is in providing an effective stimulus: one that will set their imaginations working. While, for example, the first picture in 8.4.1 could lead on to this activity (for example, a conversation between the woman who is looking out of the window and another person in the room, whom she wishes to persuade to come and look too), the stimulus is a weak one compared with the picture below, where a dialogue between the two people – and probably an emotionally charged one – is implicit in the picture. A general discussion, of the situation therefore to suggest some of the

angles from which the dialogue can be built up (e.g. *Why is the man annoyed? What do you think his wife has cooked? What do you think she says? Does the man eat his supper or not?* etc.) together with an indication of useful language (e.g. expressions of intention, of annoyance, and in particular vocabulary items connected with food) should be sufficient preparation before the students are divided into their groups. The visual stimulus might, however, be supplemented with an audio one in the form of a recorded dialogue, which the students listen to once or twice. This has the advantage of bringing the situation alive for the students.

A possible model dialogue for this situation is given below:

MRS FRY: What's the matter? Don't you want it?
MR FRY: Fish and chips again! I'm tired of fish and chips!
MRS FRY: It *used* to be your favourite meal.
MR FRY: Yes, but not three times a week!
MRS FRY: Three times a week! Rubbish! You haven't had it for over a week.
MR FRY: Well, I still don't want it.
MRS FRY: Well, in that case you'd better go and cook your own supper. And
         I'll have the fish and chips.

The following procedure is suggested for this type of activity:

Step 1   Show the students the picture (with or without a recorded version of the dialogue). Discuss the situation shown in the picture with them along general lines (getting the students to give their ideas) and provide them with some useful language (as suggested above).

Step 2   Divide the students into groups and ask them to discuss their ideas. This step is important because it gets them to *use* language. Visit the groups and advise on language difficulties. Let the students write their dialogues down when they have elaborated them in sufficient detail.

Step 3   Re-form the class and let each group present their dialogue. These can then be compared and discussed.

Step 4   (Probably in a later lesson) Let the students rehearse their dialogues in their groups, but preferably without learning them off by heart. All the students may take turns in doing this. The aim should be to get the students to act out the situation, using appropriate language spontaneously.

Step 5   Re-form the class and let each group choose students to act out their interpretation of the situation.

Note that additional situations for producing dialogues can normally be derived from the one established as above. For example, the two people in this situation would be quite likely in real life to tell someone else what had happened. Thus Mrs Fry might talk to a neighbour, while Mr Fry might tell a friend at work about it. These two possible situations may therefore be used as alternative or additional group activities. These activities also provide natural contexts for reported speech, which is often practised artificially in the classroom.

8.4.3
Picture sets for
discussion

By a set is meant a number of pictures (photographs, drawings, cutouts from magazines) which are assembled (e.g. on a large piece of paper) so as to present a topic from different angles, both providing the students with facets that can be talked about one by one and pointing out contrasts which are calculated to provoke discussion.

Let us imagine, for example, that we want to start a discussion on teenagers. Our set may provide a number of examples of teenagers today: their dress, their hairstyles, their preoccupations – and some of the things they do to annoy the older generation. At the same time it could present a contrast with teenagers in the past (e.g. in the time of the students' parents) and also underline one or two fundamental similarities. The set may also focus attention on a particular point: for example, by showing a famous – but respectable – man with long hair.

Once again, the need for careful preparation in working out the various angles from which the pictures can be exploited systematically must be

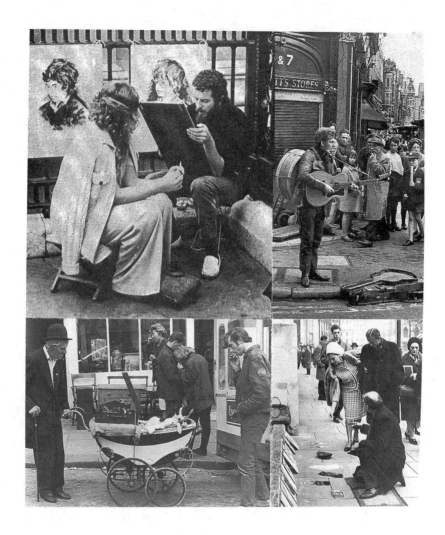

emphasised. In the set above, for example, which shows different ways of
making a living on the streets, we would first want to get the students to
identify the topic. As a starting point, they may also be asked to describe
what is happening in each picture. Then, to develop discussion, we might
focus attention on such points as *why* people do this kind of work, *how much*
they earn, whether there are certain advantages and disadvantages in it (for
example, what happens when it rains?). Your notes for this stage, then,
might well consist of a number of questions along these lines, and perhaps a
'viewpoint' (which you attribute to someone else) such as: *Some people say
these people earn a lot of money ...* However, we must also relate the topic
to the students' own background and experience. This we can do by asking
them to say, for example, which of these occupations are common in their
country, and whether there are others which are more typical, and also how
they themselves feel about these occupations: do they approve or disapprove?

Do they know anyone who earns his living in this way? Would *they* like to – and if so, which occupation would they choose?

Notice that the discussion may be either a class or a group activity. This is illustrated in the steps which are set out below.

Step 1   Prepare the class for discussion by asking the students to identify the topic and to comment on the pictures one by one (this is important, where there are a large number of pictures, to make sure that all the students are aware of what is depicted).

Step 2   Initiate discussion about the topic along general lines by asking questions or making certain statements.

Step 3   Either let the discussion continue on a class basis or else select one or two specific points for the students to discuss in their groups. For example, they may be asked to work out the advantages and disadvantages of this kind of work.

Step 4   After the groups have discussed these points and come to some conclusion, re-form the class and ask a spokesman from each group to give his group's ideas.

Related oral exercises may also be done either in groups or by the students individually. For example, the students may be asked to imagine that they have to interview one of the people in the picture and to think of five questions they would like to ask him. A dialogue can then be developed around these questions. The students may also be asked to carry out communication tasks that relate to the topic: for example, your (brother) wants to take up one of these occupations rather than a regular job. What advice would you give (him)?

Such activities, which serve to relate the topic to the students in some personal way, might normally be the final stage in exploiting the picture set. However, if time is available, the students can also be asked to work on a project in their groups: for example, an investigation of the various ways in which people earn their living on the streets (in their country), with reference, perhaps, to such things as tradition. They may also be asked to supplement the set by finding pictures of their own or to build up an entirely new set (e.g. in the form of a wall sheet, which can then be hung up for display). Much of this work can, of course, be done *out of class* in the students' own time. Its value, as an educational activity, lies in the fact that *it takes language study out of the classroom and integrates it with the students' own environment.*

8.4.4
Visual material for alternative group activities

In the three previous sections it has been assumed that you will normally be following a pattern of:

Clearly, however, there will often be occasions when you might want to do group work for 5–10 minutes, without any elaborate class preparation and without any concluding discussion of results across the class. For groupwork of this kind, individual picture cards (i.e. one for each group) provide a quick way of setting up an activity (especially if the students have done this type of activity before). Cards can be used for all three activities discussed in the previous sections: i.e. interpretation, dialogue invention and discussion of topic, and should be accompanied by a second card with instructions for the activity. For example, for an 'interpretation' activity, the group could be given the following instructions:

Discuss these questions:

1 Who is this girl?
2 Where is she? What is the town like?
3 Is the girl alone?
4 What is she looking for? (Places to visit? Somewhere to stay?)
5 Does she find the information she is looking for?
6 What does she do after this?

Now make up a story about the girl.

For a topic card, showing perhaps someone smoking or a cigarette advertisement or perhaps only a packet of cigarettes, the questions might be: *Do you smoke? (How many cigarettes do you smoke?) Does anyone in your family smoke? What is your attitude to smoking? (Do you think it is ... dangerous? anti-social? a waste of money?) Is it right to have ads for cigarettes* (etc.)?

Other uses for picture cards of this kind, particularly for informal group activities, are:

(a) *Extending the scene*

For example, for the picture of the girl looking at the tourist guide, the students can be asked first of all to invent a description of the immediate vicinity (street, square) and then the rest of the city (town, village). This activity works particularly well with pictures of rooms: the students then have to build up a description of the rest of building (what kind it is, number of rooms, the people in them and what they are doing etc.).

(b) *Association of ideas*

For this the students are given a picture of a single object and then talk about the things it makes them think of. For example, a picture of a sandwich may make some think of what they had for breakfast or what they are going to

have or would like to have for lunch. Other students may want to talk about their favourite sandwiches – or why they dislike sandwiches. Someone may have a story to tell about a sandwich. Most cards of this kind will stimulate quite a lot of talk along these lines once the students have understood the idea.

(c) *How much can you remember?*

This is a version of *Kim's Game*. The students look at the picture, which should show a scene of some kind with a fair amount of·detail, for 2–3 minutes. They then turn the card face down and try to reconstruct the scene from memory. One student should keep a record of what everyone agrees and also points of difference, and the final version is then checked against the picture. Alternatively, one student or more can look at the picture throughout, confirming or rejecting what the rest of the group say.

(d) *Find out and note*

For this one student or more has a picture card, again preferably showing a scene of some kind with a fair amount of detail, which the rest of the group have to find out about by asking questions. While they are doing this they should keep notes, which they then use to read back a description of the picture. This is then checked against the picture itself.

(e) *Roleplay*

Picture cards can be used for simple roleplay activities (see 10.3). For example, a picture of a cup of coffee could be accompanied by the following instructions for a roleplay activity: You are a group of friends at a railway station. Your train leaves in (10) minutes. A and B would like to go to the station buffet for a coffee. C wants to get on the train immediately and find seats together. D would like to get on the train but he is hungry, so he would like someone to go to the buffet to get him a sandwich. E doesn't want any coffee but he would like the others to go to the buffet so that he can get on the train and sit by himself! A few instructions along these lines are usually sufficient to get the students talking for 5–10 minutes.

8.5
Additional ways of stimulating discussion

If we think of discussion as essentially an exchange of opinions and ideas rather than the formal exploration of a topic (which is only possible at the advanced level of language learning), there are clearly many alternative ways of providing suitable stimuli. Since we need variety in our lessons, some alternatives are looked at below.

8.5.1
Texts

Topics can be effectively presented to the students through the medium of texts, which they either read or listen to. As a rule, what is required is not a text which presents the students with a mass of information but a slanted one which offers an exaggerated or one-sided point of view. For example, if the topic is space travel (assuming that this is one the students are to some extent familiar with and interested in), a text which merely describes a space mission is less likely to stimulate the students to discussion than one which questions, for example, whether we should be spending vast sums of money on space exploration when this could be better spent on projects which would improve life on earth.

Suitable material for this purpose (particularly on topical issues) can be found in newspapers and magazines (including those in the students' mother tongue), and ready-made points of view can often be taken from the 'letters to the editor' section. Columns in magazines that deal with readers' 'problems' may be used to solicit opinions and advice from the class in a realistic way.

Recorded material in the form of short dialogues, or excerpts from longer dialogues (which can subsequently be played in full to provide the actual context) can also be used to get the students to invent the situation (i.e. who the speakers are; what their relationship is; what they are talking about etc.). This is similar to the interpretation of visual material in 8.4.1.

8.5.2
Songs

The 'text' as a stimulus to discussion may be in the form of a song (which of course can be used to provide an additional or perhaps contrasting comment on a topic presented visually or through another type of text). Two songs on the same theme may also be set in contrast. There are many obvious advantages in using songs for this purpose rather than more conventional texts. They are *real* and once again provide a link between the classroom and the outside world. They are enjoyable and therefore memorable. Even if they present difficulties of comprehension, there is an incentive to overcome them. The explanation of certain lines in the song may in fact be a way of opening up discussion. And of course the active involvement of the students can be secured by asking them to join in by singing (for this purpose they will normally need a copy of the words).

A wide range of 'pop' and folk songs (which despite the natural repetition of patterns and vocabulary that they afford, could have a *bad* effect at the practice stage because deviations in grammar and pronunciation are not uncommon) can be used to explore themes – emotional, social, political – which are of direct and immediate interest to the students. Often enough the students themselves will be able to suggest precisely the songs that can be used for this purpose.

**8.5.3
Speech bubbles**

Here you provide the students with what was said; they have to decide who the speaker was; who he was speaking to and where (etc.). In other words, they have to invent a context for the utterance. This is clearly an attractive alternative to interpreting pictures: the process is very similar but speech bubbles can be easily invented and written up on the board. Indeed, the groups can be asked to write them for one another.

**8.5.4
Newspaper
headlines and
book titles**

This is similar to the activity in 8.5.3. Some examples are given below. Discussion of what the newspaper article or book is about can lead naturally on to writing (see Chapter 11 *Integrated skills*).

**8.5.5
Doodles**

The students can be asked to interpret doodles like the ones below. You can use ink blobs as well as blurred pictures (i.e. pictures that are out of focus. These can be shown on the overhead projector) in the same way.

8.5.6
Sounds

These may be individual sounds, in which case the students are asked to try to identify the object, action (etc.) or a sequence of sounds (e.g. the sound of a door being slammed, running footsteps, a car engine starting, a car moving off quickly and finally the screech of brakes), in which case the students have to invent the situation.

8.6 Problem-solving activities

This label has been used to group together a range of activities which require the learners to find 'solutions' to problems of different kinds. Many of these problems involve processes which we commonly use in real life: for example, we frequently hypothesise *links* between two things (events, actions, people etc.); we detect *differences* (real or imaginary) and we *grade* things according to criteria (subjective or objective). Here the learners are required to perform tasks which use these mechanisms in a more concentrated fashion. In the next chapter, many of the same processes will be used in gamelike activities.

8.6.1
Linking activities

(a) *Finding connections*

Here the students have to establish (i.e. detect or invent) connections between two items (presented to them verbally or in the form of pictures). For example, two such items might be *horse* and *book*. Some possible connections are:

(i)   The horse is famous because it has won lots of races, so its owner has decided to write a book about it.

(ii) The horse belongs to a man who likes reading and riding. When he goes for a ride on his horse, he often takes a book with him to read.

(iii) A man was sitting under a tree in a field, reading a book. A horse began to come towards him. The man was afraid, so he got up and ran off, leaving his book. When the horse went away, he went back into the field and got his book.

Notice that the connection between the two items can be stated very briefly as in the first example. However, the students can then be asked to elaborate on it: i.e. give the horse and the man names; say something about the races and perhaps give the book a title. Connections can also be presented in the form of little stories, like the third example.

The students may also be asked to link abstract items (e.g. *happiness* and *travel*) or more than two items (e.g. *tree, danger, school, white, run*). The latter activity is particularly suitable for getting the students to invent stories.

(b) *Finding differences and similarities*

The students may be asked to find differences and similarities as two separate activities or as part of the same activity.

For example, the students can be asked to find the differences (either a set number or as many as possible) between two pictures like the ones below, where a number of different features have been deliberately built in. For example: in the second picture, the hands have fallen off the clock; there isn't a piece of paper on the ground near the little boy (etc).

For a version of this activity in the form of a game, see 9.3.1(b).

If the students are being asked to find similarities, use unedited pictures such as photographs of streets, beaches (etc.) with quite a lot of action.

Alternatively, the students can be asked to list both similarities and differences. Pairs of words are preferable to pictures for this so that the students can talk about the items in general without being tied down to any particular presentation. For example, for *office* and *classroom*, they might start as follows:

Differences	*Similarities*
Offices have telephones.	There are usually chairs and tables in both places.
People don't have lessons in offices.	
There is usually a lot of equipment in offices, such as typewriters, ...	Both are usually part of a larger building.
	Both are usually closed at night....

**8.6.2
Categorising
activities**

For this activity the students have either to classify items according to categories they are given or to identify categories.

(a) *Putting items in categories*

The students are given a list of (say) 15–20 items, such as *occupations (bank clerk, truck driver, policeman, teacher, lawyer* etc.) and asked to locate these under headings according to different features. For example:

> physical/mental work
> indoors/out of doors
> with people/alone (etc.)

For this activity it is not necessary to have clear-cut categories. If items do not fit neatly into one category or the other, this will provoke more discussion, although in the end the students should try to agree that it belongs to one of the two categories.

Other examples:

– *everyday objects* can be divided into essential/non-essential; cheap/expensive; imported/home-produced (etc.)
– *animals* can be divided into dangerous/not dangerous; meat-eaters/non-meat-eaters; live below ground/live above the ground (etc.)

(b) *Identifying categories*

The students are given a list of items (i.e. 15–20 items like the ones above) and are asked to identify for themselves the categories into which the items can be arranged. They may be asked to find a set number of categories or as many as possible. For example, for *clothes*, some categories might be:

worn all the year round/worn only in winter
worn over another garment/worn next to the body
with sleeves/without sleeves
single items/pairs (etc.)

Note that it is advisable to try this activity out with the whole class so that the students get the idea of identifying significant categories.

8.6.3
Grading activities

(a) *Grading*

This involves putting a list of items in order according to certain agreed criteria. For example, the students can be asked to grade the subjects they study at school on a scale from most to least difficult (interesting, useful etc.). Naturally opinions will differ, thus resulting in discussion.

Criteria for other items may call for knowledge. For example, the students can be asked to arrange a list of countries on a scale starting with the largest, richest, most industrial, most densely populated (etc.).

Other sets that could be used for this activity are:

- *materials* (e.g. cardboard, copper, cotton, grass, ...): expensive, useful, rare (etc.)
- *pets* (e.g. canary, cat, dog, donkey, ...): interesting, easy to look after, unusual (etc.)
- *food* (e.g. biscuits, bread, butter, cake, ...): essential, cheap, good for the health (etc.)
- *insects* (e.g. ant, butterfly, bee, caterpillar, ...): beautiful, useful, fast (etc.)

On a more personal level, the students can be asked to rate TV programmes, films, books, pop singers, actors and actresses (etc.).

(b) *Deciding on priorities*

This is similar in that the students have to put in order of priority (or, if preferred, identify and then put in order of priority) the qualities they would expect to find in people: e.g. a friend; a husband/wife; a bank manager; a policeman; a tourist guide; a prime minister (etc.) or the features that they would expect to find in things such as a house, a car (etc.). They can also be asked to put in order of importance facilities for institutions such as a school, a social club (etc.).

Normally the students should be given a list of relevant items. For example:

friend: reliable, clever, amusing, attractive, well-informed, affectionate, kind, helpful, considerate, good-tempered.

8.6.4
Planning activities

These involve making decisions but, unlike the decision-making activities at the pre-production stage (see 7.2.4), where the students *first* made decisions, usually independently of one another, and *then* talked about them, the activities in this section are designed to get the students to *talk in order to arrive at decisions*. (Of course, in a general way, many other activities in this chapter involve making decisions too.)

The activities in this section can be presented in a relatively simple way (i.e. they do not require a lot of explanation in order to set them up, nor do they generally need any support materials) and can be comfortably done in a group session of 20–30 minutes. To exploit the full potential of other planning activities it is best to treat them as projects or mini-projects (see 11.4).

(a) *Planning a picnic*

For this the students have to decide: when, where and how to go; what to take (food, drink and other things) and what to do. Similarly, the students can be asked to plan a party. This can also involve deciding who to invite.

97

(b) *Planning a park*

The students are told that a site has become available in the centre of the town. They have to decide what facilities they would like their park to have (e.g. tennis court, swimming pool, football pitch, children's recreation area, flower beds etc.) and also where they would like these sited. Similarly, they can be asked to decide what use they would like to make of a site that has become available either in the centre of the town or on the outskirts. For example, they might like to consider: a sports centre, a parking site, a shopping centre (etc.).

(c) *Planning a club*

The students are given a simple plan of a building, like the one below, and are asked to decide how they would like to use each room, taking into account its relative size and position and also, of course, the facilities they would like their club to have.

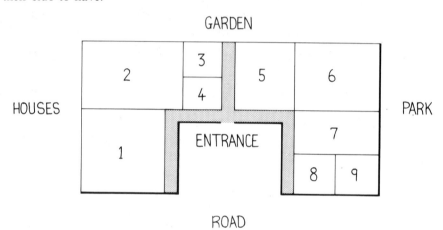

Other activities of this kind are:

 – deciding how to arrange furniture in a room or in a house;
 – planning a camping holiday: in particular, deciding what equipment to take;
 – planning a visit to a city: i.e. what to see and in what order;
 – planning how to improve their town: i.e. with regard to traffic, shopping facilities, recreational facilities (etc.);
 – planning a zoo: i.e. deciding which animals can be placed next to which. This will require a layout of the zoo and a list of animals. See *The Bus Game* in 9.3.2 (c) for a similar activity.

**8.7
Conclusion**

Although we have not yet explored all the possibilities for getting learners to talk, it is useful at this point to draw attention to the two main factors in promoting fluency, which is our main aim at this stage:

(a) *the importance of letting the students work in groups* This can be done formally or informally, depending on the type of activity, the time available and classroom conditions, but the students will need *some* opportunities to work on their own, in a face to face environment which allows them to talk directly to one another and gives them the chance to express their ideas freely.

(b) *the need to provide appropriate activities* There are two points here. First, the activities must be appropriate to the level of the students. Although we cannot and should not try to predict all the language the students will need for these activities, we should try to select activities which are *roughly* at the right level, especially in the early stages. Some relevant language can also be introduced when the activity is being presented. In the early stages this is not likely to spoil the students' enjoyment or to downgrade their efforts at communication. They will still have to work hard at the task! Secondly, we must try to select activities which are likely to involve the learners. This may involve trying activities out on a whole class basis, to attempt to gauge reactions. It may result in abandoning what we know (or believe) to be sound ways of developing fluency. However, the extent of the learners' involvement and enjoyment in an activity is a good guide to its learning effectiveness and potential and will help us decide which activities to reject and which we can make use of a number of times.

Discussion

1 What is your opinion of groupwork? Do you agree that it is essential for fluency work?
2 If you had a class of students who disliked working on their own in groups, how would you convince them of its importance?
3 In your opinion, which of the activities described in this chapter are most likely to motivate adolescent learners?

Exercises

1 Examine any textbook to see what opportunities the learners are given for fluency work. Is groupwork recommended as a procedure?
2 Assemble a set of pictures (e.g. cutouts from magazines, photos, cartoons, drawings) which could be used to stimulate a discussion on one of the following topics: (a) work (b) war (c) women in society (d) urban problems.
3 Write a set of lesson notes for discussion on the picture set: *Making a living on the streets* in 8.4.3.
4 Find suitable 'texts' for discussion from newspapers and magazines, as suggested in 8.5.1. Say why you have chosen these and how you would use any one of them.
5 Select five songs (traditional, folk, 'pop') which could be used to stimulate discussion as suggested in 8.5.2.
6 Write other speech bubbles, newspaper headlines and titles of books for exploitation along the lines suggested in 8.5.3 and 8.5.4.

References

1 On the use of visuals, see: A Wright (1976); A Wright in K Johnson and K Morrow (eds.) (1981).
2 For group activities, see: S Holden (ed.) (1978); J Willis (1981) Ch 17; P Ur (1981); A Maley and A Duff (1982) Chs 3 and 4; W Rivers (1983) Ch 3; P Hubbard et al (1983) Ch 6; J Harmer (1983) Ch 8; S Krashen and T Terrell (1983) Ch 5; A Matthews et al (eds.) (1985) Ch4.

9

Games

Games may be defined as a *form of play governed by certain rules or conventions*. They are meant to be enjoyed – wherever they are played. In the language classroom, however, games are not just a diversion, a break from routine activities. They must also contribute to language proficiency in some way by getting the learners to use language in the course of the game.

Games can do this in two main ways:

(a) *they can be used to improve the learners' command of a particular item or items of language*: sounds, vocabulary, spelling, grammatical items or functions. Games of this kind are concerned with *accuracy* and their purpose is to reinforce and possibly extend what has already been taught.

Most traditional language games fall into this category. They have been contrived or adapted to provide repetition (often frequent and rapid) of a particular item or items in an enjoyable context. They are effective because the learners are so involved in playing the game that they do not realise that they are practising language items.

Most traditional games are also *competitive:* one of the players is trying to win either for himself or on behalf of his team. And, although we do not want students to become excessively competitive, it has to be accepted that this can provide an impetus for using language with a purpose: the players in the game *want* to have a turn; they *want* to stay in the game (if this is one that involves elimination); they *want* to be the first to guess correctly or they *want* to gain points (and so on). These are, in fact, some of the mechanisms that serve to take their attention off the form of what they are saying and make it possible for us to introduce the element of repetition.

(b) *they can be used to provide the learners with opportunities to use language rather than simply practise it:* that is, they are concerned with *fluency* rather than accuracy. Such games normally involve *a task* of some kind: in order to complete the task, the learners have to use language, often as best they can in the circumstances. In this respect they are similar to the activities described in the previous chapter. They differ not because they are more enjoyable – because other types of activity can or should be equally enjoyable – but because they are played according to a set of rules.

Two devices are frequently used in this type of game:

(i) *the 'information' gap* This, in its simplest form, means that A knows something that B does not know. B's task is to 'bridge' the gap by acquiring that information. A may share it with him or B may have to elicit it.

(ii) *the 'opinion' gap* Again, in its simplest form, A has a certain idea or opinion and would like to persuade B that he is right. A's task, then, is to bridge the gap by stating his point of view effectively.

Traditional language games also make use of these two mechanisms, of course. Guessing games, for example, depend on an information gap, and in many other games the player's contribution has to be evaluated.

Note that for information gap type games (see *Describe and draw* in 9.3.1 for example) the players normally *collaborate*: that is, they work together in some way in order to complete the task, often by sharing the information that each has. In this respect, these games are not 'won' in a conventional sense; they are successfully completed. For opinion gap activities (see *Use it* in 9.3.2, for example), the players often *compete* to some extent. A player can gain points if he can persuade the other players of something and this will probably help him to win the game.

Both types of game clearly have their place in language learning. The first type, with its focus on accuracy, belongs mainly to the practice and pre-production stage. These games provide new contexts for rapid and enjoyable practice in many key language areas – areas so essential, such as tenses or sets of lexical items, that the learners need a massive amount of practice, both initial and for periodic revision. The second type, on the other hand, with its focus mainly on fluency, belongs to the production stage and thus provides a new dimension to the activities already discussed in Chapter 8.

9.2 Accuracy-focussed games

These are normally played with the whole class, often with the students divided into teams. They can then be played in pairs or small groups for additional practice on a greater scale. However, since the purpose of these games is to reinforce or extend the learners' command of specific language items, your main task will be to monitor the performance of the students by, for example, deciding who is right, giving points for correct answers (etc).

The following general procedures are suggested for this type of game:

(a) Choose games carefully on the basis of suitability both in terms of language and with regard to the students themselves (e.g. their age and interests). The size of the class may also have to be taken into account.

(b) Explain the game carefully, in the mother tongue if necessary.

(c) Give the students one or more 'trial runs': that is, try the game out on a 'let's-see-how-it-works' basis, so that you can sort out any problems.

(d) Involve as many students as possible. Although you may be at the centre of the game at the start, let the students take over from you as soon as possible.

(e) If games are being played on a team basis, give points for each correct answer and write the scores up on the board.

Examples of these games are given below, mainly with a view to highlighting the principles on which they are based.

9.2.1
Games involving variation of an item within the same structure

(a) *Guessing games*

The majority of repetition games rely on the simple but productive device of getting the players to find out something through guessing. Examples of this type of game have been given in 5.4.1.

At the most elementary level we have guessing games such as *What's in the box?* or *What have I got in my bag?* in which the learners try to guess the name of an object by asking: *Is it a . . .?* or *Have you got a . . .?* At the intermediate level we might use an imaginary situation in which the person who is answering questions (you or one of the students) pretends that he has forgotten to buy something while he was out shopping to elicit: *Did you forget to buy (+ item)?* Or, at the advanced level, the students might be asked to try to find out what somebody would have been doing if he had not come to class by asking: *Would you have (gone to the cinema/been sleeping*? etc.).

In short, to exploit this device to the full, all we need to do is:

– *adjust the language to suit the needs of the class*. The *What's in the box?* game could be played to practise: *It might be . . . /I wonder if . . . /Could it possibly* be . . .?

– *think of a suitable context or setting which will involve the learners*. Food items, for example, can be practised within the context of situations such as shopping, meals, likes, dislikes and preferences.

Since guessing games usually go at a brisk pace, they can be played with the whole class, with the students taking turns to find something out. They can also be played in teams.

(b) *Sentence-building games*

The traditional version of this game is: *I went to the market and I bought . . .* The first player completes the sentence with an item (e.g. *a loaf of bread*); the second player repeats that sentence and adds another item (e.g. *. . . bought a loaf of bread and some bananas*) and so on. However, we can not only vary the structure within the same context (e.g. *When I go to the market, I must buy . . . /If I had gone to the market, I would have bought . . .*), but also use different contexts. For example:

– When I go on holiday, I'm going to take . . .
– While I was walking down the street, I saw . . .
– For my birthday, I was given . . .
– When they cut him open, they found inside . . .

Phrases can also be added instead of words e.g. *While I was walking down the street, I saw a man breaking into a shop (a woman waiting for a bus* etc.).

Sentence-building games can be played with picture cues e.g. flashcards which are shown only once, (the players have to recall all previous items) or wall pictures, where the players have to select for themselves the items which they want to use. Because of the excitement they generate, these games are very appropriate for team work.

9.2.2
Games involving a variety of structures

Here the context of the games encourages a wider use of language, but still with the overall aim of promoting accurate command of the items being used.

(a) *Guessing games*   Once again, one of the key mechanisms used is getting the students to try to find something out by guessing. Some examples are given below:

(i) *Twenty questions*

For this, one player 'thinks' of an object; the others try to find out what it is by asking not more than twenty questions, normally of the *yes/no* type (e.g. *Is there one in the room? Is it (yellow)? Can you (eat) it?* etc.). Unlike the guessing games in 9.2.1, the players are trying all the time to narrow the field either by eliminating certain possibilities or by picking up clues to the object. The game therefore calls for much more skill and careful listening. Usually the players will have to be given some indication of the nature of the object. For example, they might be told what category it belongs to (animal, something found in the house, an action) or some other type of clue: e.g. *It's small and it's made of metal.*

(ii) *What's my line?* That is, what job do I do?

For this, one of the players chooses an occupation and the others try to find out what it is by asking questions. As for *Twenty questions* the number of questions may be limited and again are normally restricted to the *yes/no* type. For example, the players may ask: *Do you work (indoors)? Is your job (hard)? Do you earn a lot of money?* (etc.) Players may choose their own jobs (but preferably from a list, otherwise the game may prove to be frustrating) or be given a picture card showing their occupation. They may also be asked to mime an action connected with their work before the game starts.

(iii) *'Glug'*

For this, one of the players thinks of a verb; the other players try to find out what it is by asking questions in which an invented verb (*glug* or *diggle*, for example) is used as a substitute for the unknown one. For example:

A: Are you glugging now?
B (*who has chosen the verb* wash): No.
C: Do you glug a lot?
B: Quite often, yes.
D: Do you like glugging?
B: I don't mind it!
E: Do you glug before you come to school?
B: Of course!
F: Have you always glugged?
B: Yes. For most of my life. (etc.)

The questioning continues until the players are able to guess the verb. Notice that in the course of the game they have to use a variety of verb forms e.g. tenses, infinitives, gerunds.

Note that for all these games, where the players are trying to guess their way 'towards' the answer, you can involve some of the class as 'audience'. That is, instead of participating in the game by asking questions, some students are told the answer and listen while the rest of the class try to guess.

```
┌─────────────────────────────┐
│        ANSWERERS            │
└─────────────────────────────┘

┌──────────────────┐  ┌──────────────────┐
│                  │  │                  │
│    LISTENERS     │  │   QUESTIONERS    │
│                  │  │                  │
│                  │  │                  │
└──────────────────┘  └──────────────────┘
```

(b) *Elimination games* For these games players have to stop playing if they do not make a correct response. Two examples are given below.

(i) *Simon says*

One player gives a number of commands. If he prefaces these with *Simon says* (e.g. *Simon says* 'Stand up'), the other players have to carry them out. If he gives the command on its own (e.g. *Stand up*), the other players should do nothing. The game needs to be played briskly, in order to try to catch players out (i.e. make them carry out the instruction when it is not prefaced by *Simon says* . . .) Large classes can be divided into groups, which take part in turn. The winners from each group are then allowed to take part in the 'finals'.

(ii) *True or false?*

The players have to repeat a statement if it is true. This can be done with reference to a picture. For example, the person in charge of the game (you or one of the students) shows a flashcard or points to a wall picture and says: *She's running* or: *He's wearing a black hat*. The players say nothing if this is not true.

Since it is not always easy to detect if a student is saying nothing (when he ought to be confirming that a statement is true), this game is best played with the class divided into small teams. As for *Simon says*, the winners are then allowed to take part in the 'finals'.

(c) *Memory games* The most basic form of this is *Kim's game*, for which the players have to try to recall a number of objects which they have been allowed to see for a short time (e.g. 1–2 minutes). However, for a wider and more interesting use of language, you can use, for example, a wall picture, with a number of things happening. The students, preferably divided into teams, make statements from memory about the picture. For example: *There were two birds in the sky. A man was sitting under the tree* (etc.). For variation, you (or students from opposing teams) can make true/false statements about the picture which must be accepted or rejected. For example:

T (*to Team 1*): There were two birds in the sky.
A (*Team 1*):   That's correct.
T: Good. (*To Team 2*) The birds were black.
B (*Team 2*):   That's correct.
T: Do you agree, Team 1?
C (*Team 1*):   No. They were grey. (*etc.*)

9.3
Fluency-
focussed games

For these games the students will normally work in small groups. Some activities (e.g. *Describe and draw*, *Find the difference*) could be done in pairs, but this will involve the preparation of material on a greater scale. If you have a large class of thirty of more students, divide them into three groups and ask students to work in pairs within the group (e.g. taking turns, sharing decisions). This makes the game go at a faster pace. For some activities you

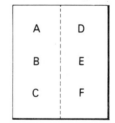

may want to divide the group into two sides. For example, for *Describe and draw*, you will have one student describing the picture; the others (who cannot see the picture) drawing. For *Find the difference*, the two sides can be equal.

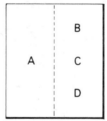 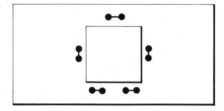

Describe and draw   *Find the difference*

The following guidelines are suggested for these activities:

(a) *Select the appropriate game*   The game should put the players under pressure to communicate, but it should not be so far beyond their linguistic level that they find it frustrating, thus causing communication to break down.

(b) *Explain the game carefully*   Each game is governed by a set of rules, which the players must follow. You can present these orally to the class, using the mother tongue if necessary, or you can make them available in self-access form (see below).

(c) *Provide adequate rehearsal*   This will be necessary the first time the students play the game. Subsequently, they should be able to play it without further instructions from you.

(d) *Monitor the students' performance*   That is, go round and listen in as for other group activities. The players should feel free to consult you (although they should not ask you to act as judge), but in general do not interfere with a game while it is in progress.

(e) *Provide feedback*   You can tell the students how well they have done if that is appropriate. This can be done on a class basis. Normally, however, you should make use of what you have learned of the students' performance while monitoring to shape your future teaching.

(f) *Keep a record*   This should cover both what games they have done, how well they did them and what their reactions were to them. You should also keep a note of any ideas you get for variations on the games.

If you want to make the games available to the students on a self-access basis i.e. so that they can select for themselves which ones they want to do in a particular lesson and get on with it without any further guidance from you, you should put the material to be used in cardboard or plastic folders or envelopes, with instructions on the outside. It is important that the instructions should be clearly set out, as shown in example below, step by step. If necessary, these instructions could be in the mother tongue.

DESCRIBE AND DRAW

Instructions for Player A

READ THESE INSTRUCTIONS CAREFULLY!

1   You will find a picture in this envelope. Do not show it to the other players.

2   Tell the other players that they will need paper, pencil and a rubber.

3   Describe the picture. You may give a general description first. Tell the players to draw what you describe. They may also ask questions. Do not look at what they are drawing.

4   When the players have finished drawing, show them your picture. Compare pictures and discuss any differences — and problems.

Examples of games are now given.

9.3.1 Information gap games

All three games described below are collaborative: that is, the players have to work together, sharing information in some way in order to complete the task.

(a) *Describe and draw*

In this game, as you can see from the self-access rules in the previous section, one player has to describe to the other player(s) a picture which they are not allowed to see. Those who are listening have to draw the picture. They may ask questions for clarification (if there is more than one person drawing, they must listen to one another's questions) and they can discuss any difficulties amongst themselves. Further talk takes place when pictures, the original and the various versions of it, are compared.

This need not be an advanced level activity provided the pictures to be drawn are reasonably carefully selected. Pictures, which may be taken from magazines or be drawings which you have produced yourself for the students, can be unusual but should not contain distracting detail. Clearly, however, this is a game which requires language to be used precisely. You can give the students a preview of this activity in class by doing what is commonly called a 'picture dictation'. See 3.4.2(c).

(b) *Find the difference*

For this the players, divided into two sides, each have pictures which are similar to one another but differ in a number of significant details (see the pair of pictures in 8.6.1(b), for example, which could be used for this game). The players have to establish the differences between the two pictures (either as many as possible or a set number) by describing or asking questions. For example:

A: There's a boy in my picture. Is there a boy in yours?
B: Yes. He's in front of the window. It has 'buffet' on it.
A: Buffet? That isn't on my window. What's the boy doing?
B: He's looking at the ground. Yes, he's looking at a piece of paper.
A: Oh, there isn't a piece of paper in my picture. Where is it?
B: It's . . . near his feet . . . (etc.)

(c) *Complete it*

For this each player (or pair of players, since they can 'share' a picture) has a picture. Each picture either shows the same scene from different angles or forms part of a sequence of events, as in the example below (which is in fact simply a picture composition cut up and shared among the players). The players, who cannot of course see one another's pictures, talk to one another until they have built up the complete story. They then show one another their pictures so that they can check their version of it.

Player A

Player B

Player C

Player D

Here is an example of how the four players might talk to another while they are trying to work out what the picture sequence is about:

A: Well, I've got a picture of a man with a beard. He's an artist. And he is showing a woman a picture he has painted.

C: Is it a picture of the woman?

A: Yes – and she's very ugly! She doesn't like the picture!

C: Ah, in my picture the man – the artist – hasn't painted the picture. He is just going to paint it. The woman is sitting in a chair . . .

D: It's funny . . . in my picture the artist has also painted the picture of the woman – but in the picture she's very pretty!

B: Yes, she's pretty in my picture too – and she's showing the picture to some friends.

A: I don't understand it. Did he paint two pictures?

B: Yes . . . I think I understand it. First he painted a real picture of her – I mean she was ugly in the picture too . . .

D: Yes, and she didn't like it, so he painted another one. But he made her beautiful this time.

C: All right. Let's try and work out the story. I'll start . . .

Any type of picture sequences (cartoon, composition) can be used for this purpose. Each picture should be mounted on cardboard and kept in an envelope.

9.3.2
Opinion gap games

(a) *Use it*

For this game you need two sets of picture cards (like those in 7.2.1(c)). The cards in the first set show or symbolize occupations. It is preferable on the whole to use symbolic cards because the players are then free to choose their own occupations provided that they are consistent with the pictures. For example, *pencil* might be interpreted as standing for: teacher, clerk, writer, artist (etc.). The cards in the second set show objects which the players have to make use of in connection with their occupations. Both sets are placed downwards on the table in front of the players.

Each player takes an occupation card and decides what his job is. The players then tell one another what they are (i.e. this information is not *secret*!). Each player in turn then takes one of the object cards and says how he would use it in his work. If the other players are satisfied with what he says – and sometimes a good deal of comment and questioning takes place – the player is allowed to keep the card. If they do not accept his idea (i.e. if he cannot bridge the opinion gap by convincing them), he must put the card back on the table.

The game depends a good deal on how imaginative and resourceful the players are in inventing uses for the objects they pick up rather than the level of language. For example, if the player who has chosen the occupation of teacher picks up an object card which shows a box of matches and cannot find an 'obvious' use, he might say: *I need them because I am nervous and I smoke a lot* or: *I need them to burn homework with!*

Word cards may be used instead of picture cards.

(b) *'Desert Island'*

A controlled version of this game (where the players kept more or less to the same pattern: *I'm going to* ...) was described in 7.2.3(b). However, the full potential of the game is exploited only if the students are allowed to use language freely. It is important that the players should argue with one another about their choices and the reasons they give for them. For example:

A: What have you decided to take, B?
B: Well, I think I'll take a gun, a clock and a pen ...
C: What are you going to do with the gun?
B: I can shoot things ... animals, birds ... and I can protect myself.
D: Can you use a gun?
B: No, but ... Well, I can make a noise with it.
A: Yes, when a ship comes near. What about the clock?
B: I want to know the time, of course.
E: Why? It isn't important on the island.
C: And you have the sun. You can tell the time with the sun.
B: Yes, but I want to have a clock. It's like a friend.
D: What about the pen? (etc.)

Notice some of the many ways of playing this game:

(i)   Different places may be used. For example: *hospital, camping site,* ... *the moon*!
(ii) The cards may be placed face downwards on the table. Each player takes a card without knowing what the object is.
(iii) The players take one object at a time and say what they would do with it. The card is then placed face downwards and cannot be used by any other player.

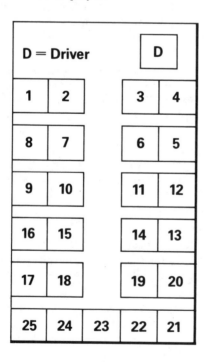

(c) *The Bus Game*

For the basic version of this game (referred to in 8.6) the students will need a board divided up to represent the seats on a bus, with the driver at the front, as shown in the diagram. You will also need a set of 'passenger' cards (showing at least the faces of the people and their names). Some of the passengers should be related: e.g. you might have a family consisting of Mr and Mrs Smith and their son, Tom. The cards are divided up among the players, who then take it in turns to seat their passengers on the bus. Each player must say, therefore, where his passenger is going to sit and why. For example:

A: Mr Ball wants to sit next to Mrs Smith.

B: Why?

A: They are old friends. They haven't met for a long time. And now Mr Ball wants to talk to Mrs Smith.

C: But Mrs Smith is going to sit next to her husband.

A: No, she doesn't want to sit there. She wants to sit at the back of the bus.

B: But where is Tom Smith going to sit?

A: Oh, with one of his friends probably. I don't know. Anyway, he can't sit there because Mr Bell is going to sit there!

As for other opinion gap games, each player must try to convince the others that he is right.

Some variations of this game are:

(i) A mixture of animal and people cards may be used as passengers. The players have to work out an acceptable way of seating them.

(ii) After the passengers have been seated on the bus, an object card is placed face downwards under each passenger. The players then take turns to pick up an object card and to try to explain why the passenger has that object with him.

Note that for all opinion gap games, it is a good idea to get 2–3 students in each group to act as a panel of 'judges'. Their task is to listen carefully to all the opinions put forward and to decide if they are acceptable. The judges may also be asked to award points on a scale of 1–5.

9.4
Board games

We have already seen how board games can be used to practise structures and vocabulary (see 7.2.3). They can also be adapted to provide opportunities for free expression.

The principal skills involved are:

– listening and speaking: the players have to listen to one another in order to participate in the game.

– reading: normally the players will have to interpret the rules for the game.

Overall, board games have good motivational value: this is a 'real-life' activity that has been brought into the classroom.

Most boards can be used for a variety of purposes. For example, the shopping and places boards in 7.2.3 can be both used for fluency-type activities. For the shopping game (perhaps with more shops added to the board), the players can be asked to say why they have to buy something from each of the shops or to tell a little story about something that happened to them in each shop. For the places game, they can be given the name of a country (etc.) and asked to say three things about it.

Three types of board are illustrated and discussed below. All are easy to make. Pictures of objects are best used for the first one, but words can be used instead.

(a) *Type 1*

For this board we have adapted the picture set in 7.2.2, although perhaps the board should be slightly larger (i.e. 25 squares).

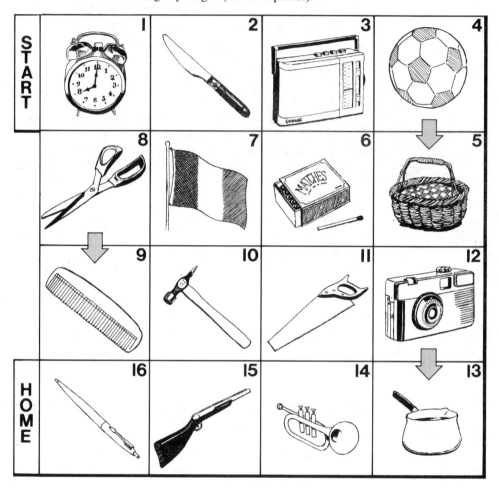

As the players move round the board, they can be asked to:
- state a use for the object they land on;
- state a 'normal' use and an 'unusual' one;
- state a connection between the object they land on and the object they have moved from;
- say what they will do with the object if they are allowed to keep it.

These are 'opinion gap' tasks, of course, so the players have to convince one another that they should be allowed to move. The winner can be the player who gets the most points when the game stops (i.e. after an agreed number of dice throws or an agreed time).

(b) *Type 2*

This type of board game consists of a continuous track, with as many squares as you like to put on it. Some squares have large dots on them. These represent 'penalty' squares: if a player lands on one of these, he has to carry out a task of some kind, either from a prepared list or from one given to him by one of the other players. The list of tasks can be written on a piece of paper and numbered, so that the players have to take them in order, or they can be written on cards, which are then placed face downwards on the table. The advantage of having the tasks in the form of cards is that they can be added to or withdrawn.

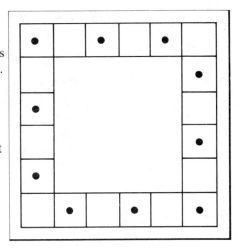

Some examples of tasks are:

- the players may be asked to give the names of (six) countries, animals, sports, illnesses (etc.). Note that in this case the spontaneous use of language comes not so much from the task itself but from the interaction between the players while the task is being carried out. This is, of course, a feature of many games.

- the players can be asked to carry out instructions e.g. draw a picture, sing a song, perform an action (etc.).

(c) *Type 3*

This is another open-ended board game which can be put to different uses. It consists of a numbered track, with a S(TART) and a H(OME), which the players have to follow. If they land on a circle, something pleasant or advantageous happens. If they land on a triangle, something unpleasant or disadvantageous happens.

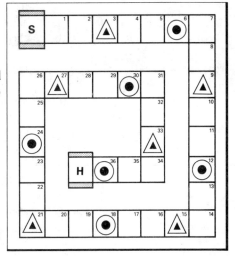

The 'good' things and 'bad' things depend on the context of the game. For example, the players may be trying to get to some treasure that is located in the centre of the board (i.e. where HOME is marked). The circles help them to move forward: e.g. they represent a short cut, a lift, a good road (etc.). The triangles are obstacles: e.g. there are rocks on the road, wild animals, floods (etc.). The conditions attaching to each of these (e.g. move forward/back 2/3 squares etc.) must be agreed beforehand.

To make full use of the board, therefore, you must invent different contexts or situations in which good or bad things happen. Some examples are:

– you are escaping from your kidnappers (or having a dream about escaping!);
– you are on a camping/boating holiday;
– you are saving up to buy a (motorbike).

A list of 'events' then has to be worked out for each situation. This can be done with the help of suggestions from the class. Alternatively, the students can be asked to work in groups to write their own lists, which they then give to another group to use.

Discussion

1 Do you agree that language games are an important way of giving oral practice to learners of all ages and at all levels?
2 In your opinion (and experience), is there a place for both types of games (accuracy-focussed and fluency-focussed) in the average classroom?

Exercises

1 Examine any textbook to see what use is made of games (of either type). Decide whether they form an integral part of the unit or whether they are mainly decorative.
2 Suggest other items that could be practised through the sentence building game in 9.2.1(b).
3 Give other examples of accuracy-focussed games that you have found useful in the classroom.
4 Write out a list of rules, similar to those for *Describe and draw* in 9.3, which could be used to make any of the other games in the following sections available on a self-access basis.
5 Suggest alternative ways of using the board games described in 9.4.
6 Devise or adapt a language game of your own and say how you would play it with the class.

References

1 For a detailed analysis of games, with examples, see S Rixon (1981).
2 For a wide range of games, see A Wright et al (1984).
3 For information and opinion gap games, see D Byrne and S Rixon (1979).
4 For other examples of games, see:
– S Holden (ed.) (1978);
– H Moorwood (ed.) Section 7 (1978);
– A Maley in K Johnson and K Morrow (eds.) (1981);
– S Holden (ed.) (1983b) Section 6.
5 For many of the games described in 9.3 and 9.4, see D Byrne *Interaction Package B* (Modern English Publications 1978) and *It's Your Turn* (Modern English Publications 1980).

10

Drama

Drama is used in this chapter as a generic term to cover the following activities:

(a) *mime*   The participants perform actions without using words (although, as we shall see, this activity leads naturally on to 'talk').

(b) *roleplay*   The participants interact either as themselves in imaginary situations or as other people in imaginary situations.

(c) *simulation*   This involves roleplay as defined above. However, for this activity the participants normally *discuss a problem* of some kind with a *setting* that has been defined for them.

Each of these activities is discussed and illustrated below. One thing that they all have in common, however, is that they involve *fantasy:* they contain an element of *'let's pretend'*. Some of the situations used may be *realistic* – perhaps they have been chosen because they are ones in which the learners will or are likely to find themselves – but they are not *real*. They are make-believe and, to take part, the learners have to imagine they are somewhere other than the classroom. In this respect alone they are important because they help us to escape from the classroom on an imaginative level.

But dramatic activities do more than that. They also provide yet another range of opportunities for the learners to develop fluency skills: to use language *freely*, because they offer an element of choice; to use language *purposefully*, because there is something to be done; and to use language *creatively*, because they call for imagination. Thus viewed, then, they complement other types of fluency work we have looked at so far.

Where they differ, however, from other kinds of fluency activities is that they get the learners to *behave through language*, not simply *talk*. They help to develop communication skills within the broader framework of social behaviour.

At this point we also need to be clear about what drama in the language classroom is *not*. It is not, for example, 'acting' in the sense of performing before an audience. The skills we are trying to develop are communication skills, not acting ability. We may of course invite the students to do their mime or roleplay for other students to see, and the students may get a certain satisfaction from this; but this is a means to an end, a way of getting more talk and discussion. The *process*, however, is more important than the *product*. Secondly, drama does not, for the most part involve working from a scripted text (i.e. as in a play, where the characters have 'lines' to say). Interpreting – and in exceptional circumstances, performing with the help of – a text is just *one* kind of dramatic activity and needs to be seen within the context of other work.

10.2 Mime

Miming – performing actions without using words – may not at first sight seem directly relevant to the development of oral ability. Indeed, it might seem more appropriate as a language game – which of course it can be if someone mimes an action and the others try to guess what it is.

Our goal here, however, is not to develop the ability to mime in itself (that is, to make the students more proficient at expressing themselves without using words, although this can sometimes be a useful skill in foreign language 'survival' situations), but to make them aware that there is more to communicating than simply using 'words'. We also use facial expressions (to show or conceal our feelings). We use gestures, mostly unconsciously and far more than we realise. The way we stand and move is also significant, and likewise the way we react to people we are talking to. By trying to get the learners to communicate through actions alone, either in situations where language is not normally used or where it has been filtered out (like turning down the sound on TV), we can help focus attention on these features and make the learners aware of their importance first in roleplay situations (see 10.3) and ultimately when they come to use language in 'real life'.

Activities for developing this kind of language 'awareness' can be very simple. For example, we can ask the students, working in pairs or small groups, to mime actions such as these: eating something; reading something; making something; breaking something; cutting something; moving something; watching or waiting for something – or somebody. The 'something' (or 'somebody') is a very important ingredient of the activity: *what* we are eating will determine to a great extent *how* we eat it, together with how we feel at the time, both in respect of the object (e.g. whether we like it) and independently (e.g. whether we are hungry, in a hurry etc.). For all activities of this kind it is essential, therefore, for the students to have a clear and precise idea of what the object is and how they feel about it. This in itself will be a natural source of 'talk' when the learners tell the others about the object afterwards. But first the other students in the group will naturally want to try to guess, to comment and perhaps then say how they would have done it. 'Wordless' activities, then, lead quite naturally to 'talk'.

Other miming activities, which might perhaps be best regarded as 'roleplay without words' because they involve situations where language would naturally be used, are:

(a) ask the students to work in situations where there are not only actions but also probably some show of feelings. For example:

- two people sharing a table
- two people sharing some food
- two people sharing an umbrella
- two people sitting next to one another.

For all these situations the participants have to decide *where* they are (e.g. the table could be in an office, library, restaurant); *who* they are and what their *relationship* is.

(b) ask the students to work in small groups (e.g. of 5–6) meeting one another

- as themselves
- in different roles e.g. friends/strangers
- in different moods e.g. cold/friendly
- with different reactions e.g. surprise, fear.

(c) ask the students to work in larger groups (e.g up to 10) interacting with one another first as themselves, then as someone else in situations such as:

- meeting at a party
- waiting in the doctor's waiting room
- standing in the foyer of a cinema or theatre before the show begins
- walking around in a public square.

For all these activities the students should work first with mime (that is, to see how well they can project themselves and their feelings without using words) and then use talk appropriate to the situation. All activities should be followed up (and in some cases preceded by) discussion.

10.3
Roleplay

Roleplay, like other dramatic activities, involves an element of 'let's pretend', but as we noted in 10.1, we can offer the learners two main choices:

(a) they can *play themselves in an imaginary situation*. For example, they can be told:

> You are standing at the entrance to the school.
> A passer-by asks you the way to the nearest
> (supermarket). Give him the necessary directions.

Both participants can be themselves (although the 'passer-by' would of course know where the supermarket is). They are also familiar with the setting: all they have to do is to project themselves into it.

(b) they can be asked to *play imaginary people in an imaginary situation*. For example, they can be told:

> A is a suspicious-looking character waiting at night behind a supermarket. B is a policeman, who finds him there. B decides to arrest A, who protests and tries to explain what he is doing there.

Not only is the situation fanciful; it can also be said that the students are unlikely ever to find themselves using English in the roles of policeman and possible burglar!

These are two deliberately extreme examples: the first a very ordinary situation; the second a piece of fantasy. They raise, however, some important questions. First, what kind of roleplay situations should we use or make the most use of – *realistic 'everyday'* ones which the learners are likely to find themselves in, or *fanciful 'fun'* type ones which are remote from experience? There is, unfortunately, no easy answer to this question. Clearly we should make use of some realistic situations, especially if we can predict fairly accurately which ones are likely to be relevant to the learners, so that we can feed in some useful bits of language (e.g. ways of asking for and giving directions for the first example above). However, 'fun' type situations may prove to be far more stimulating and, besides, two astronauts discussing how to spend a free afternoon will provide a context for making suggestions no less than two people planning a picnic. In the end, perhaps, we should decide in the light of which situations the learners prefer.

No less crucial is the question: should we ask learners to be themselves or to play the part of imaginary people? In many roleplay situations we have no choice but to ask some participants to play the part of imaginary people. For example, if you want the students to use language in the context of buying and paying for something in a shop, *somebody* has to play the part of the shopkeeper. Clearly, then, we have to compromise: students will sometimes have to play roles that are not relevant to them in order to play ones that are. One of the drawbacks of realistic-type situations is that they often involve roles such as shopkeeper, policeman, receptionist (etc.).

What is more important, perhaps, is that we should recognise that some learners feel more comfortable as themselves or perhaps cannot project easily into other roles, while others are happy to take on another role either because they are more outgoing or because they are happy to shelter behind the mask of other people.

For roleplay to be successful, then, we need not only to identify situations which will stimulate the learners but also give them roles that will match the requirements of their personalities. Unlike activities which we have discussed so far, roleplay involves the learners *on a personal level*, and the more choice we allow them to create their own roles and to develop their own situations, the less risk there will be of forcing roles on them which they are reluctant or unable to fulfil.

10.3.1
Establishing
roleplay situations

This brings us to the question of how we define roleplay situations for the learners, which of course we must do to some extent. In fact, we have already considered some possibilities in Chapter 8, when we looked at various ways of stimulating self expression through visual and other material. The task of creating a dialogue in 8.4.2 is essentially a roleplay situation. A roleplay task was also suggested in 8.4.1 in connection with the second picture: persuade someone to help you do the washing-up. For this, one student would have to identify with the woman in the picture; the other role or roles would have to be defined.

In general, as we have noted, it is important to give the learners an element of choice: they must be free to choose *something* for themselves, either what they say or how they interpret the situation.

Some ways of providing a framework for roleplay practice are looked at below.

(a) *Open-ended dialogues*

This term is used for dialogues which leave the learners free to decide how to develop them. For example:

A = assistant in a bookshop
B = customer

A: Hello. Can I help you?
B: Well, I'm looking for a copy of . . .
A: Do you know the author's name?
B: . . .
A: Hm. I'm pretty sure we haven't got a copy.
    Would you like me to order one for you?
B: . . .
A: . . .
B: . . .

Thus the dialogue provides a frame for *beginning* the roleplay, which is often difficult for students. The student playing the part of the customer has only to choose or invent the author and title of the book. How the roleplay continues, however, is left to the participants. The customer might ask the assistant to check whether he has the book; ask how long it would take for the book to arrive; decide for or against ordering the book (etc.).

Generally speaking, this is a satisfactory way of setting up a simple roleplay at the elementary to intermediate levels, especially for 'survival'-type situations. The dialogue can be written up on the board; ways of developing it might be discussed and the students should not need to look at the text when they do their roleplay. And since there are likely to be many different interpretations – students might like to be themselves as customers or create parts and they will certainly think up a variety of outcomes for the situation – they will be naturally curious to see what others have done.

(b) *Mapped dialogues*

We have already looked at these in 7.2.1 (e), in connection with controlled mini-dialogue practice. The example is reproduced here with the 'functional' cues for each speaker on separate cards, so that there is an 'information gap' between them. We shall also need to define the relationship between the two speakers: e.g. they are friends.

1 Invite B to go out with you 2 Suggest another possibility 3 Confirm arrangements

1 Decline 2 Accept 3 Agree

This presentation is superficially attractive because the speakers will want to bridge the information gap and they also have to provide all the language for themselves. Their moves, however, are controlled throughout (and any attempt to make them more open only makes the activity more complicated by presenting too many choices) and at the same time some learners find it difficult to work from instructions presented in this way.

(c) *Role instructions*

These describe the situation and tell the participants how they should interact. For example, we might re-present the bookshop situation as follows:

You go into a bookshop to buy a book. (Describe author and title.) Ask the bookseller if he has the book. If the book is not available, decide whether to order it.

Examples of possible items of language may also be included. For example:
I'm looking for ... /Have you got ...?/I wonder if you have ...

Together with the open-ended dialogue in (a), this seems to be an effective way of setting up a roleplay situation especially since the instructions can be very simple, yet at the same time leave the learners free to choose the language they would like to use.

(d) *Scenarios*

These outline the sequence of events (like the description of a play or film) without giving any of the words used. The events could of course be presented through a series of pictures (like a picture composition sequence).

Scenarios can be about everyday realistic-type situations like the one below:

> A went into a cafe. There was rather a long queue. A wanted to look at the menu, but B was standing in front of it. So A asked B to read the menu to him. A made various comments as B did this.
>
> A decided to have a salad. The salad section was located further along the counter. A asked a number of people for permission to pass.
>
> A picked up his salad and went towards the cash desk. On the way, he passed C, who was carrying a tray of food. A bumped into C and knocked the tray out of his hand.

A scenario of this kind is clearly intended to encourage the students to use functions such as asking for and giving information, asking for permission and apologising, but in addition to that there is also room for talk of a general kind – and of course some fun. The scenario below, which is of the fantasy kind, also involves the use of everyday functions such as giving instructions and making suggestions (see the possible 'conversation' below) but calls for a more imaginative interpretation.

> A railway carriage. An elderly couple follow a porter, who is carrying their suitcases, along the corridor towards a compartment. The porter finds an empty compartment and puts their suitcases on the luggage rack, where there is one other small suitcase. The couple sit down and the train leaves. They hear a loud ticking coming from the small suitcase. The noise alarms them and they throw the suitcase out of the window. A man comes into the compartment and sits down. He looks towards the luggage rack for his suitcase ...

For roleplay activities based on scenarios, notice what the students, working in groups, will have to do:

(i) *They will have to decide where 'talk', either obligatory or optional, occurs.* For example:

- the couple talk to one another as they walk along the corridor;
- one or both tell the porter where to put the suitcases;
- one or both talk to the porter as they pay him;

– they talk after they sit down;
– they discuss the noise they hear;
– they decide what to do;
– they talk after they have thrown the suitcase out of the window;
– the man says something when he sees that his suitcase is missing.

(ii) *They may want to modify the scenario in some way*. For example, they may decide to have a family instead of a couple. Other minor roles, such as people looking into the compartment and deciding not to stay, may also be introduced.

(iii) *They will need to work out what (they think) was actually said*. They may need some guidance (this is something you should normally decide before they start), but generally they must be encouraged to work at their language level. Here is an example of a possible text to show how they could do the roleplay in quite simple language.

PORTER: Ah, here's an empty compartment. Where shall I put the luggage?
OLD MAN: Put the big suitcase up there (*points*) and the other one up there. Thank you very much. Here you are (*giving money*).
PORTER: Thanks.
OLD LADY: Listen! Can you hear a noise?
OLD MAN: It's coming from that suitcase. Oh, it's only a clock.
OLD LADY: No, it isn't. It's too loud! Perhaps it's a . . . bomb!
OLD MAN: What shall we do? Call the guard? Stop the train?
OLD LADY: No, let's throw it out of the window!
OLD MAN: All right. Open the window! There!
OLD LADY: Well, that's better . . .
MAN: Hey, where's my suitcase?

(iv) *They have to decide about the characters*. For example:

– exactly who they are
– what they look like
– where they are going (etc.).

Likewise they must have a clear idea about the setting. These aspects are very important in helping to bring the roleplay alive.

(v) *They must decide how they are going to do the roleplay*. For example, who is going to play which parts and what 'props' they are going to use (e.g. perhaps schoolbags for suitcases).

All these stages will involve a good deal of natural discussion, no less important than actually doing the roleplay itself. This of course is the final stage and the students will no doubt want to show their interpretations of the scenario to one another. As for other roleplay activities, this should be done in as relaxed a way as possible.

10.3.2
Scripted roleplay

This title is used for any roleplay activity that involves interpreting a text in the form of speech – from the apparently simple (and not always exciting) textbook dialogue to a scene from a play. Except when it is done on a very superficial level, this kind of activity is far from easy: the learners not only have to bring the text alive – translate it from printed words on a page into speech – but also work out an interpretation that is consistent with the text.

Other types of roleplay considered so far have allowed the learners to 'create' their own text, which, even allowing for language problems, is on the whole easier.

(a) *The textbook dialogue*

This (especially if it is the presentation dialogue in a unit) is normally treated from a narrowly linguistic standpoint. The main function of such a text is, after all, to convey the meanings of language items in a memorable way. Of course we may also ask the learners to practise saying it together (see 4.4.3 Step 9) or even to 'act it out' in front of the class, but we will probably be satisfied at this stage if they reproduce adequately the interpretation they have been exposed to, through a recording or your reading aloud. Clearly this activity does little to deepen their understanding of the text as an example of *people behaving through language*.

We cannot of course explore in depth every sample of speech our students are exposed to, but we can stress the importance of looking beyond the words printed on the page and the cardboard figures who speak them. We can do this by getting the students to:
- make the setting as 'real' as possible (over and beyond what is provided in the coursebook, which is sometimes minimal);
- think about the relationship between the characters;
- suggest how the characters might stand and move while talking. Although dialogues do not usually involve a lot of movement, the speakers are unlikely to be completely inert!
- suggest appropriate facial expressions and gestures;
- suggest feelings and attitudes.

Some of this may have to be done in the mother tongue. It can, however, be a very revealing exercise to take even a simple mini-dialogue like the one below and to get the students to explore not just different ways of 'saying' it but also how they relate to the factors listed above.

A: How about going to the cinema?
B: All right, if you like.
A: You do want to go, don't you?
B: You know very well I love going to the cinema.

The same process can be applied to any textbook dialogue and is an important preliminary to interpreting longer texts such as plays or scenes from plays.

(b) *Plays*

Dialogues are a pedagogical convenience – a way of presenting learners with relevant samples of spoken language. The approach we have suggested brings them a little closer to plays, as these are normally understood. Plays are meant to be 'done', rather than said or read; they are intended to be performed in front of an audience. And we have already stated that performing in front of an audience is *not* one of the *aims of* roleplay.

If, then, we use plays in the language classroom with our students, performance should be incidental, unless *they* want to perform (normally only in front of one another) and if we have time. If the students enjoy putting on a scene, then they will almost certainly learn something from it. Our task is to:

(i) *select the material carefully*. We need to ensure that it is manageable both in terms of language and length (whether it is original, adapted or specially written);

(ii) *exploit the process that leads up to any performance*. That is, get the learners to discuss the setting, the characters (their personalities, their relationship etc.) and how the scene should be done. In this respect, the approach is the same as for any other kind of roleplay activity, except of course that good original material is likely to be more educationally valuable. The process of interpretion will therefore be correspondingly more challenging and instructive.

What, then, of play reading? This is really a special kind of activity in its own right. It is also done outside the classroom as an alternative to an actual on-stage performance – generally without any audience and with the minimum of movement. Its goal, however, must be to interpret the text, not simply to read it aloud.

Since the learners are unable to bring to this activity the same kind of intuitive understanding of the text that might be expected of native speakers (who in any case normally study and think about their parts beforehand, so that their performance is far from spontaneous), play reading needs to be approached with care if the students are to derive any real benefit from it. The following procedures are suggested. Steps 7–9 take us a little beyond play reading to the point where the students are acting out their interpretations of the play.

Step 1   Ask the students to familiarise themselves with the text (play or scene) by reading it through on their own.

Step 2   Read the text aloud to the class or, if at all possible, play a recording of it.

Step 3   Discuss the text with the students, inviting their ideas about the setting, the characters and their relationships (etc.).

Step 4   Assign roles to the students. You can give the same role to more than one student (especially if it is a long part) so that everyone is involved from the start.

Step 5   Read or play the recording a second time, pausing to draw attention to or invite comments on, for example, the way certain utterances are said, and what attitudes or emotions are shown in this way. Discuss also the way the characters interact.

Step 6   Ask selected students to come to the front of the class (so that they can be easily seen and heard) to read. Let other students take over as appropriate.

Step 7   Divide the students into groups. Ask them to discuss the setting and the characters in detail (i.e. to try to establish their own interpretation as far as possible). They can read the play as they do this, assigning roles on a provisional basis.

Step 8   (In a later lesson) Ask the students in their groups to choose their roles and rehearse the play.

Step 9   Ask the groups in turn to act out the play (or a scene from it). The other students should listen critically and be prepared to comment on the performances afterwards. If possible, make a recording of the performances for the students to listen to later.

**10.4
Simulation**

A simulation has already been defined as an activity where the learners discuss a problem (or perhaps a series of related problems) within a defined setting. Let us look at a simple example to see what this involves. The students might be told:

> A social club is in financial difficulties. A decision must be taken to close it down or keep it open.

To resolve the problem, a meeting of some kind must be held. This could be a committee meeting, in which case the participants will be restricted to members of the social club committee. A setting of this kind would be suitable for small classes. Alternatively, we could have a public meeting, attended by representatives of the social club committee and members of the public. This would enable us to involve a large number of students – even a class of thirty or more, as we shall see below.

So far, however, the activity is scarcely different from a discussion or debate. To transform it into a simulation we must:

(a) *establish the setting by providing background information* about the community and also the club and its problems. The club itself could be for young people, with either a mixed committee of adults and adolescents or run by adolescents alone. Either possibility would appeal to secondary-school students. Some possible background information might be:

– a report on some of the club's activities with details of money earned or lost;
– a newspaper article about the club and its problems (i.e. condensed information);
– a conversation between (two) people talking (mainly) about the club (to provide information that the students have to pick out).

This background information will consist mainly of texts to be read or listened to. We might also want to include visual material in the form of pictures of the club, maps, diagrammatic information (etc.).

(b) *define the roles of the participants.* We noted earlier that the students can roleplay themselves or other people. For this simulation we can provide roles of both kinds. For example, we shall need to ask a number of students to perform 'official' roles such as chairman of the meeting, club secretary, club treasurer, committee member(s) in charge of the activities programme and perhaps the local youth officer. Such roles, which require the students to play the part of someone else, will all have to be defined fairly carefully.

Other students will have to act as members of the public. We could have a completely teenage public (in effect, members of the club), in which case students can be themselves with the minimum of role definition. For example,

125

one member of the public could be instructed to intervene by attacking the club on the grounds that it wastes money. Another might be instructed to come up with a solution for saving the club. Yet another might be invited to adopt any attitude he likes.

Generally speaking, the participants will need rolecards which will not only give them a new name but also give them some tasks to perform. These tasks will give the simulation some direction by ensuring certain lines of interaction. For example:

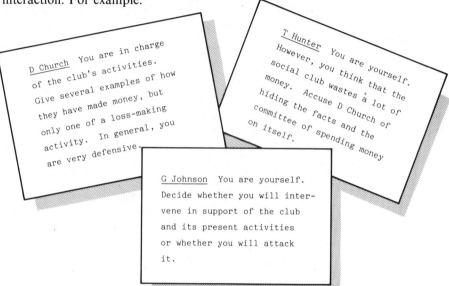

D Church You are in charge of the club's activities. Give several examples of how they have made money, but only one of a loss-making activity. In general, you are very defensive.

T Hunter You are yourself. However, you think that the social club wastes a lot of money. Accuse D Church of hiding the facts and the committee of spending money on itself.

G Johnson You are yourself. Decide whether you will intervene in support of the club and its present activities or whether you will attack it.

If we have a large class (thirty or more students), it is unrealistic, however, to give all the students actual or potential speaking roles (even if some of the roles are minor) because they will not all be able to contribute at the actual simulation stage (although they can be involved at a pre-simulation group discussion stage). One way of involving all the students simultaneously is to devise some roles with listening tasks. These listeners will, in effect, be reporters of some kind: they attend the meeting as representatives of the press, TV, radio and other interested bodies. Their function is to listen, take notes and later use these notes to write articles and reports.

GENERAL PUBLIC Major and minor roles

COMMITTEE Major speaking roles

REPORTERS Listening roles

We can identify the following main stages in developing, presenting and doing a simulation.

Step 1 Construct the 'scenario': that is, define the problem and the setting.

Step 2 (a) Write or adapt appropriate support materials. These must provide the students with enough information to bring the problem and its setting alive and to enable them to perform their roles meaningfully.

        (b) Write rolecards for each participant. Although these should not be too detailed, they should ensure that the participants will interact.

Step 3 Present the scenario to the whole class, together with appropriate background information. For example, at this stage they might be given a general picture of the club and its problems.

Step 4 Assign roles, taking into account the personalities and skills of the students. For example, some may prefer to have major speaking roles; others quite small roles as themselves. Again, some students will be much more effective as reporters.

Step 5 Ask the students (working individually, in pairs or in small groups) to study the background information in detail and to develop their roles. Most speakers, for example, will have to think of what they will actually say. For the simulation above, the class at some stage could work in three groups:
- the committee could elaborate on the background to the club and its activities;
- the members of the public could discuss amongst themselves what line they are going to take towards the club;
- the reporters could work out the background for their newspapers etc.

Step 6 The groups share additional information.

Step 7 Do the simulation (approximately one class period).

Step 8 Do follow-up. This can be done in three ways:
        (a) *feedback*   on the simulation itself: how well it went, discussion of problems (etc.). The students should be able to provide their own verdicts.
        (b) *project work*   For example, the simulation could be followed up by a visit to an actual social club, with interviews and reports.
        (c) *further simulations*   For example, if it is decided to save the club by raising money, one simulation might concern itself with the organisation of a scheme to raise money.

It should be noted that although, in comparison with roleplay and most forms of discussion, simulation is a relatively complex activity both in terms of the support materials needed and the stages that have to be gone through, there is nothing to prevent it being done in average classroom conditions at an intermediate level. But there are no formulas or recipes for success. Simulations may go well or badly, and this will not always depend on whether they have been carefully prepared or how well they are supported with materials (and certainly not on whether these materials are commercially produced). The real success of a simulation will depend on how well it involves the students and how effective it is in getting them to use language purposefully.

Because simulation is a relatively complex activity, your role too as manager – or 'controller' as it is usually called for this activity – will also require much more involvement. You should note the following points:

– You will probably need to explain the idea of simulations to the class: what they are and what can be achieved through them.

– You should explain your role in the simulation: that is, you will be there to see that nothing goes wrong (see below).

– You must help as required at the pre-simulation stage: e.g. you may have to define or modify roles and assist with the interpretation of support materials.

– Your main task during the simulation is to see that everything goes smoothly. Much of the help you will need to provide will be of a 'mechanical' kind: e.g. ensuring that copies of reference material (recorded or written) are available at the right stage. You may also need to intervene indirectly in a discussion: e.g. if you see that someone is talking too long, you can 'arrange' for someone else to interrupt. As for other activities of this kind, you must also be available for consultation: e.g. if the participants cannot resolve a problem, they can say: 'Well, let's ask the controller'. For them, the controller should be a *real* person, not just the teacher in disguise!

– When the simulation is over, you should lead the follow-up discussion. A major aim here is to get the students to evaluate the simulation in general (particularly what they learned from doing it) and their own performance in particular. At the same time you can use this opportunity to point out any mistakes you noted during the simulation. Finally, try to get the students themselves to suggest possible follow-up work in the form of projects or further simulations.

Discussion

1 Do you agree with the definition of drama in this chapter to include simulation?

2 In your experience (of learning or teaching a foreign language) do you think that roleplay is a valid activity for learners of all ages and levels? Do you think that some learners find it difficult to project themselves into imaginary situations?

3 Do you agree with the basic procedures suggested for play reading? If not, what modifications would you like to suggest?

4 Do you think that simulation is too complex an activity in average classroom conditions?

Exercises

1 Examine any textbook to see what use is made of roleplay activities. In particular, decide whether enough guidance is given and whether the personality of the learners is respected.

2 Suggest other activities involving the use of mime.

3 Write a cuecard similar to the one in 10.3.1(a) which could be used for setting up a roleplay situation through an open-ended dialogue.

4 Write a scenario similar to one of those in 10.3.1(d) (i.e. decide whether your scenario is mainly functionally oriented or of the 'fantasy' type).

5 Write a short play (about 50–75 lines long) based on the scenario about the railway compartment.

6 Write rolecards similar to those in 10.4 for participants in the public debate on the social club.

References

1 On the use of drama in the classroom in general, see:
– S Holden (1981);
– S Holden in K Johnson and K Morrow (eds.) (1981).
A valuable background book (not specifically concerned with foreign language teaching) is: J Seely (1976).

2 On roleplay, see:
– G Sturtridge in K Johnson and K Morrow (eds.) (1981);
– C Livingstone (1983);
– W Littlewood (1981) Ch 5.

3 On simulations, see K Jones (1982).

11

Integrated skills

There is a tendency in language classrooms (although perhaps a diminishing one) to focus attention on one skill at a time: thus, in one lesson, or part of a lesson, special attention is paid to oral work; in another to reading and so on. This sometimes reflects the apparent needs of the learners. Often, however, it is a pedagogical convenience rather than a necessity and probably reflects the way skills have been sequenced in the unit of work in the coursebook: speaking/listening → reading → writing. This kind of sequencing recycles and reinforces language items, but does not integrate skills in any real sense.

Notice that in 'real life' we do not use language skills in any set order or in any necessary conjunction with each other. For example, if we see an interesting advertisement in the paper for a holiday, we may discuss it with somebody and then perhaps ring up or write for more information. This nexus of activities, which so far has involved reading → speaking/listening → either speaking/listening or writing, may continue or stop at that point. It can provide a model for integrating skills in a realistic way and is especially useful at a post-elementary level. It is briefly illustrated in 11.2. Another simple but effective way of ensuring that skills are integrated is to get the learners to collaborate, in pairs or in groups, on many of the fluency-focussed tasks described in the previous chapters (see 11.3). Finally, both simulation and project work provide a natural framework for integrating skills. Project work is described in 11.4.

First, however, we need to see why integrated skills activities are important:

(a) They provide opportunities for *using* language naturally, not just *practising* it.

(b) Many pair- and groupwork activities call for a variety of skills, sometimes simultaneously, in order to involve all the learners.

(c) Students seem to learn better when they are engaged on activities which involve more than one skill.

We are not of course suggesting that single-skill activities are not effective: there will in fact be many occasions when we shall ask the students just to talk or read or write, because this is appropriate. Equally, however, we should be looking for opportunities to knit skills together, because this is what happens in real life.

11.2
An integrated skills sequence

For this we will return to the example in 11.1.

1 *Tom is reading the paper. He sees this advertisement for a holiday.*

2 *Tom shows the advertisement to his wife. She reads it.*

TOM: What do you make of it, then?

ANN: Well, it sounds a bit odd to me ...

TOM: How?

ANN: Well, it's so cheap, I mean. You couldn't get a week's holiday at home for that money.

TOM: Yes, but holidays in India *are* cheap. At least ... Anyway, I think I'll ring up and find out more about it.

ANN: Well, you can't ring. There isn't a phone number. I told you it was odd!

TOM: Well, in that case I'll write ...

3 *Write the letter which Tom sent to Gita Travels. Say where you saw the ad. Begin* Dear Sir, ... *and end*: Yours faithfully, ...

Here, then, we have the beginning of a sequence that could lead on to a whole range of activities. For example:

– Tom gets a letter from Gita Travels, asking him to ring up or call in.
– Tom discusses the letter with his wife. He decides to visit the agency because it is quite near his place of work. (The students make up the dialogue.)
– Tom visits the agency, where he meets Mr Somu. Mr Somu gives him more details of the holiday (orally or in writing). Tom is interested. (The students are given the opening lines of the dialogue, then roleplay Tom and Mr Somu.)
– Mr Somu asks Tom to fill in a form and pay a small deposit (etc.).

Notice that, through this type of activity, the students not only roleplay the characters in the story (which provides a context for these activities) but also contribute through talking or writing. The students may also be given options e.g. Tom may question Mr Somu about the form; he may fill it in there or take it away to discuss with Ann (etc.).[1]

11.3 Activities

These activities show you how you can integrate skills through the simple expedient of getting the learners to work in pairs or groups. This introduces a 'talk' component into the normally silent activities of reading and writing. You should note how purposefully the skills are used in this way: the students talk, read or write *in order to get something done*.

(a) *Questionnaires*

See 7.2.5 (a) for details. Two students collaborate on the production of the questionnaire (i.e. talk and write). They then separate to use the questionnaire. This interviewing stage also involves talking and writing (i.e. filling in the questionnaire). The original pairs then unite to compare results. At this stage, then, we have reading and talking.

(b) *Quizzes*

See 7.2.5 (b) for details. Again the students collaborate (in pairs or groups) on the production of the quiz, so that we have talking and writing. The quiz may involve some reading in the form of research or checking of information. The quiz is then passed to another pair or group, who read, talk and write. Finally the quiz is passed back to the students who wrote it, so that we get reading and talking.

(c) *Describe and note*

This is a variation on the game *Describe and draw* in 9.3.1 (a), where one student describes a picture which one or more students try to draw, asking questions as they do so. For this version, the students who are listening make notes, asking questions if they want clarification. They then compare notes. Finally they use their notes either to describe the picture orally or to produce a written description.

(d) *Draw the picture*

Two or more students collaborate to produce precise instructions needed for drawing a picture or map. This involves detailed discussion leading to writing. These instructions are then passed to other students, who read, talk and then draw. The two pictures are then compared (leading to more talk).

(e) *How much can you remember?*

See 8.4.4 (c) for details. The students, working in groups, look at a picture for 1–2 minutes before turning it face down. Then, either individually or in pairs

---

1 For further examples of this type of activity see: Donn Byrne and Susan Holden: *Going Places* (Longman 1980) and *Follow It Through* (Longman 1978).

(the latter involves more talk), they write down what they can remember. They then compare their notes and use them to produce an oral or written description of the picture. Finally, they turn the picture over and compare it with their version.

(f) *Stories*

This can take two forms:

(i) The students work in groups to produce a scenario, as in 10.3.1 (d), which is then exchanged with another group for roleplay work.

(ii) The students work in groups to produce two short stories (each 4–5 sentences long), which they then mix up to form one text. The 'jumbled' stories are then exchanged with another group, who have to work out the two original stories (i.e. read, talk and write).

11.4
Project work

Some teachers regard any activity which involves individual or group research over a period of time as project work. Very often this kind of activity is topic-centred and results in the production of a piece of written work. Other teachers attach more importance to activities which will get the learners out of the classroom, particularly those that involve the collection of data through interviewing. There are, in fact, no neat definitions of project work. It can be both individual and collaborative; it can be done in or out of the classroom (depending on the nature of the project and other constraints) and it may or may not result in a substantial 'product'. *Something* must be produced – but the emphasis may be more on the *process* than the product itself.

Clearly the important thing in the foreign language classroom is to identify project work which, in narrow terms, will provide a framework for language use and development that is satisfying and effective. It should be something that the learners enjoy doing and find purposeful, while its effectiveness derives a great deal from the way it integrates skills naturally. At the same time, on a broader front, project work will require and help to develop skills which are equally important (although often neglected) in the mother tongue. They are:

– communication skills (when interviewing and reporting back);
– research skills (when reading);
– social skills (when discussing, collaborating, meeting people etc.).

Sometimes for project work students will have to work through the mother tongue (see below), but this need not concern us if the outcome is educationally beneficial.

Projects have to be carefully planned, through a process of teacher-learner collaboration, but their setting up, as well as the guidance and monitoring that is needed in support, is largely a matter of common sense. Things may go wrong, as with other activities, particularly those on a large scale like simulations, but because of the involvement demanded, project work must not be allowed to collapse or result in frustration. Your role is crucial: in identifying or helping to identify project areas; in providing adequate support and in motivating the learners.

A long-term project, such as the one discussed below, which would result in the production of a class newspaper/magazine ('newsmag') would involve the following stages:

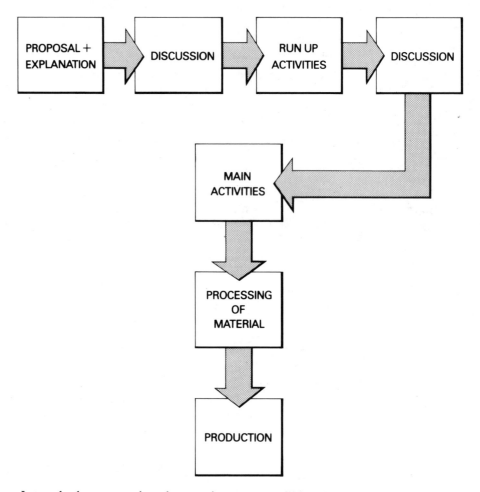

Let us look now at what these various stages will involve.

Step 1   *Present the project to the class* and explain what you have in mind – and what the project may involve. The main aim here is to create a positive atmosphere towards the idea.

Step 2   *Get the reactions of the class to the idea through discussion.* This will probably result in identifying two areas which will need detailed discussion:

Tasks: What do we need to know in order to carry out the project? Tasks will be done at the 'run up' stage, which normally involves a lot of research.

Problems: What sort of difficulties are we likely to come up against? For example, time, money, organisation.

There is no set way of going about this. You may like to have a 'brain-storming' session with the whole class and, having identified as many tasks and problems as possible, divide them into groups to discuss one task (or problem) or to discuss each of them. Alternatively, you may prefer to keep all discussion at the class level for the moment. Probably it is better to do some groupwork at this stage, sharing out tasks and problems according to skills and interests.

It has to be acknowledged that the students will sometimes find it difficult to do all the work at this stage in English. We need to compromise, therefore. The proposal and explanation of the project should be done in English as far as possible, together with any class discussion (because *you* can help out with the language); but, if necessary, for the sake of getting the learners involved and getting the project started, groupwork could be done in the mother tongue.

Step 3   *Organise the class for the 'run up' activities.* This particular project would involve a large number of these, both in and out of the classroom. The main activities would be interviewing and reading. For example:

–   *visits to newspapers and magazines*: finding out how they are run and about related services (e.g. printing) and interviewing staff;

–   *reading about the history of newspapers and magazines*;

     comparing newspapers and magazines: both in English and the mother tongue;

–   *analysing newspapers and magazines*: e.g. content, structure, roles (editor, reporters etc.);

–   *raising money*: possible sources (auction, fund-raising, donations, advertisements etc.).

Note that the first four items are tasks; the last one is a possible problem. However, it may not be necessary to raise money at all if the project is supported by the school or if the newsmag is produced very cheaply (e.g. cyclostyled, not printed).

How should the various tasks be divided up? The visits to one or more newspaper offices should probably be treated as a 'class outing'. It would be educationally valuable in itself and motivating as a whole for the project. The interviewing of staff, on the other hand, is a separate venture and should be done by a selected group of students. Similarly, the other tasks are best shared out.

Step 4   *Ask the students to report on their research so far.* Most of the tasks at the 'run up' stage will have been done in the mother tongue (e.g. the visit to the newspaper office – unless there happens to be an English language newspaper near at hand. Similarly, reading material on the history of newspapers (etc.) may not be available in English at the right level). However, the 'reporting back' as well as the writing up of any notes should be in English.

Step 5   (a) *Ask the students to decide on the final form of their 'newsmag'.* Having gained some experience of the 'real thing' (through visits, reading etc.), the students are now in a better position to decide what sort of newsmag they would like. This may call for some more groupwork. However, the students must now make up their minds what kind of material they would like to have in their news-mag and, as far as possible, which students will produce the material.

(b) *Ask the students to prepare material for the newsmag.* Some possible areas are:

– *articles and reports* (e.g. surveys (on local problems), events, interviews);
– *creative writing* (stories, poems);
– *reviews* (books, records, films, plays, concerts, TV programmes, computers);
– *fun features* (crosswords, puzzles, jokes, cartoons, games, competitions);
– *letters* (to the editor, agony column);
– *advertisements* (real, fictitious);
– *special topic areas* (sport, science, pop music);
– *illustrations* (photos, drawings).

In effect, what the students are doing at this stage is to prepare, over a period of weeks or perhaps months, in and out of class (as homework, if necessary) the 'copy' that will be needed for the newsmag. The preparation of this material should involve as much discussion as possible and should also be done collaboratively wherever possible. There are, however, no 'rules' and some learners will naturally want to work on their own, giving their undivided attention to writing. Nevertheless, they should be encouraged to consult one another for ideas and opinions and also to have their material checked.

Step 6   *Get the students to process the material.* At this stage the newsmag has to be given some sort of shape, taking into account the material that is available. That is, the material has to be allocated (perhaps provisionally) to specific pages. This is best done with the whole class. For example, divide the board up into sections (one for each page of the newsmag) and get the students to suggest and agree where to site the material. Then divide the class up into groups and give each group responsibility for working out the layout of one or more pages. This will involve a good deal of discussion, some editing (i.e. purposeful summarising) and perhaps some exchange of material with other groups until a satisfactory page layout is achieved. It is also possible that some new material (text or pictorial) may be needed to fill in some pages. If there is too much material of a certain kind (e.g. sport), this could be turned into a special supplement.

Step 7　*Get the students to produce the final version of the newsmag.*　There is not a great deal that can be usefully said about this final stage – the actual production of the newsmag – except of course that it is vital for it to take place, otherwise all the preceding activities are pointless. Students must feel that they are working towards a *real* goal. It is not the actual *form* (which will already have been decided) that matters: a series of wallsheets, with typed articles and hand-drawn illustrations (and costing almost nothing) may be just as satisfying as a professionally printed newsmag. What is important is that the students should be able to *see* and *show* the final product to which everyone has contributed.

Not all projects need be as elaborate as the one described in this section (see 8.6.4 for examples of mini-projects). However, it is valuable from time to time to undertake an activity which not only integrates language skills but also goes on throughout much of the term or school year. This project also integrates work in the mother tongue and English (the students have to do some purposeful translation) and, last but not least, the classroom and the 'real world'.

Discussion

1 Do you agree with the importance attached to integrated skills in this chapter?
2 What is your view of project work? Do you think it is too complex an activity to be carried out in average classroom conditions? (If you think this, can you suggest a more modest approach to project work?)

Exercises

1 Examine any textbook to see what provision is made for activities that integrate skills.
2 Write, in outline, a sequence of activities like the one about holidays in India.
3 Suggest other activities like those in 11.3 that could be used to integrate skills along the same lines.
4 Devise a project (simple or complex) which would combine opportunities for outside visits, research through reading and interviewing and a range of language skills.

References

1 On integrated skills, see D Byrne in K Johnson and K Morrow (eds.) (1981) and C Read in S Holden (ed.) (1984) for work at the beginner level.
2 For examples of integrated skills activities, see S Holden (ed.) (1983b) Section 5.
3 A useful book on project work in general is D Waters (1982).

Bibliography

ABBOTT, G and WINGARD, P *The Teaching of English as an International Language* (Collins 1981)

BROWN, G *Listening to Spoken English* (Longman 1977)

BROWN, G and YULE, G *Teaching the Spoken Language* (Cambridge University Press 1983)

BRUMFIT, C *Problems and Principles in English Teaching* (Pergamon Press 1980)

BRUMFIT, C (ed.) *General English Syllabus Design* (Pergamon Press 1984)

BRUMFIT, C and JOHNSON, K (eds.) *The Communicative Approach to Language Teaching* (Oxford University Press 1979)

BYRNE, D *Teaching Writing Skills* (Longman 1979)

BYRNE, D and RIXON, S *Communication Games* (NFER – Nelson 1979)

ELLIS, R *Classroom Second Language Development* (Pergamon Press 1984)

GOWER, R and WALTERS, S *Teaching Practice Handbook* (Heinemann 1983)

HARMER, J *The Practice of English Language Teaching* (Longman 1983)

HOLDEN, S *Drama in the Language Classroom* (Longman 1981)

HOLDEN, S (ed.) *English for Specific Purposes* (Modern English Publications 1977)

HOLDEN, S (ed.) *Visual Aids for Classroom Interaction* (Modern English Publications 1978)

HOLDEN, S (ed.) *Focus on the Learner* (Modern English Publications 1983a)

HOLDEN, S (ed.) *Second Selections from Modern English Teacher* (Modern English Publications 1983b)

HOLDEN, S (ed.) *Teaching and the Teacher* (Modern English Publications 1984)

HUBBARD, P, JONES, H, THORNTON, B and WHEELER, R *A Training Course for TEFL* (Oxford University Press 1983)

JOHNSON, K and MORROW, K (eds.) *Communication in the Classroom* (Longman 1981)

JOHNSON, K and MORROW, K (eds.) *Functional Materials and the Classroom Teacher* (Modern English Publications 1984)

JONES, K *Simulations in Language Teaching* (Cambridge University Press 1982)

KRASHEN, S and TERRELL, T *The Natural Approach* (Pergamon Press and Alemany Press 1983)

LITTLEWOOD, W *Communicative Language Teaching* (Cambridge University Press 1981)

LIVINGSTONE, C *Roleplay in Language Learning* (Longman 1983)

MALEY, A and DUFF, A *Drama Techniques in Language Learning* (Cambridge University Press 1982)

MATTHEWS, A, DANGERFIELD, L and SPRATT, M (eds.) *At the Chalkface* (Arnold 1985)

MOORWOOD, H (ed.) *Selections from Modern English Teacher* (Longman 1978)

RIVERS, W *Communicating Naturally in a Foreign Language* (Cambridge University Press 1983)

RIXON, S *How to Use Games in Language Teaching* (Macmillan 1981)

SEELY, J *In Context* (Oxford University Press 1976)

STEVICK, E *Teaching and Learning Languages* (Cambridge University Press 1982)

UR, P *Discussions that work* (Cambridge University Press 1981)

UR, P *Teaching Listening Comprehension* (Cambridge University Press 1984)

WATERS, D *Primary School Projects* (Heinemann 1982)

WIDDOWSON, H *Teaching Language as Communication* (Oxford University Press 1978)

WILKINS, D *Second Language Teaching and Learning* (Arnold 1974)

WILLIS, J *Teaching English through English* (Longman 1981)

WRIGHT, A *Visual Materials for the Language Teacher* (1976)

WRIGHT, A, BETTERIDGE, D and BUCKBY, M *Games for Language Learning* (Cambridge University Press 1984)

Index

Longman Group UK Limited,
Longman House, Burnt Mill, Harlow,
Essex CM20 2JE, England
and Associated Companies throughout the world.

© Longman Group Limited 1976, 1986
All rights reserved; no part of this publication
may be reproduced, stored in a retrieval system
or transmitted in any form or by any means, electronic,
mechanical, photocopying, recording or otherwise,
without the prior written permission of the Publishers.

First published 1976
New edition 1986
Ninth impression 1994

BRITISH LIBRARY CATALOGUING IN PUBLICATION DATA

Byrne, Donn
    Teaching oral English. —2nd ed. — (Longman
    handbooks for language teachers)
    1. English language — Study and teaching —
    Foreign speakers   2. English language —
    Spoken English
    I. Title
    428.3'4'07   PE1128.A2

ISBN 0-582-74620-5

Set in 10/12pt Monophoto Times
Produced through Longman Malaysia, TCP

Acknowledgements

We are grateful to the following for permission to
reproduce copyright photographs:

Barnabys Picture Library for page 87 (top right);
Dorothy Cloynes for pages 83 and 87 (bottom left);
The Photo Source Ltd/Keystone for page 87 (bottom
right); Andrew Wright for page 87 (top left).

The photographs on pages 90 and 91 are by the
Longman Photo Unit.

We are also grateful to Modern English Publications
for allowing us to reproduce in modified form a
number of illustrations which first appeared in their
teaching materials.